PRAISE FOR *TAKE YOUR PLACE IN THE KINGDOM*

I encourage you to read Miranda Nelson's book. It will greatly enrich your spiritual journey! I've known Miranda and her husband, Jerame, for years. We have traveled across the nations together in ministry, and I am so thrilled to see how God has anointed them. Miranda has my full and complete endorsement. In this book you will discover wonderful keys which will equip you to draw nearer to God and to walk in your God-given authority!

—Bobby Conner, Founder
Eagles View Ministries

I want to highly recommend not only this amazing new book, but the life and ministry of Miranda Nelson. There are few women I know who are connected with heaven and move in the miraculous like Miranda. In her new book *Take Your Place in the Kingdom,* Miranda not only reveals hidden keys that teach you how to move in the supernatural, but she beautifully reveals her intimate relationship with Jesus Christ and how power and authority flows out of that intimate union with Him.

I've known both Jerame and Miranda for years now, both as ministers and friends, and have witnessed the amazing anointing that rests on Miranda's life. You will be richly blessed by this new book.

—Jeff Jansen, Founder
Global Fire Ministries International

This book is filled with faith, hope, and love—things that remain (1 Cor.13:13). Either it will be the dynamic faith that Miranda exhibits, the hope that flows from the powerful testimonies, or the compassionate love evidenced in the healing miracles that move you, but you will be transformed by the pages of this book. Miranda Nelson shows you how to lead a dynamic kingdom life, full of the power of God. I highly recommend it!

—Stacey Campbell, Founder
Be a Hero and RevivalNOW!

🦢 A WORD FROM SHAWN BOLZ 🦢

If you were given the rights of kingship over a country today, it would take many counselors to help you understand your privilege and authority. You wouldn't even understand the power of your position, let alone the raw authority you were entitled to. Also, since most of you reading this book have not been raised in a monarchy, you haven't experienced the culture of a kingdom of authority—where kings and queens have the ultimate authority.

In our spiritual life as Christians, we have been given an investment of authority from heaven, and that is why God has sent His Holy Spirit—the wonderful counselor—to customize our hearts to heaven's culture so that we will take our place in the kingdom. This process of learning is about more than just getting theological knowledge or practicing church-centric activities; it is literally about evolving into our identity as sons with Jesus. It is a mindset change and heart discovery. We are already spiritually full of authority because we were given the fullness of Christ, but there is a process to understanding how to walk this out here on earth—not just in empowered positions, but in a way that empowers people.

Miranda covers the very real steps to moving into your God-given rights and authority, but she keeps the effects of the kingdom of love (we have authority over) as the central theme. As she covers identity, authority vs. power, and so many other subjects, she takes you through her own intriguing story; her life and ministry have touched so many people—living pictures that will help align your heart with kingdom culture.

Our generation is preparing to take greater risks and influence every industry known to man with authority that only comes from heaven. To take this jump of faith, we have to invest in the identity that only comes from being seated with Christ and from walking in the deepest, most profound relational journey we can go on. Gifting and power cannot compel our hearts to make these faith leaps continually, but having such a connection to who God is, is what will sustain us in the place we are entitled to walk. Miranda is a picture of this in her spiritual walk and lifestyle, and she shares both from her life growth and from the strength of her current position in Christ. She proves that as you encounter God and love people, the spiritual authority that comes from your heavenly position only increases.

Having authority and walking in it are two totally different things. To walk in authority you have to understand the process, and I love how this book lays out the boldness and faith steps so you can make clear choices to take your place in God's awesome kingdom! It is your time to walk in all authority, the authority that Jesus, himself, paid for on the cross. I pray that the Holy Spirit would open your eyes as you read this book so that you too can feel "placed," both in your God-given seat of empowerment and in your identity.

—Shawn Bolz, Senior Pastor of Expression58:
An entertainment-based ministry in Los Angeles
Author of *Keys to Heaven's Economy* and other books

—————————MIRANDA NELSON—————————

Take Your Place in the Kingdom

Walk in Your God-Given Authority

——A LIVING AT HIS FEET PUBLICATION——

TAKE YOUR PLACE IN THE KINGDOM
Copyright © 2014 by Miranda Nelson

Miranda Nelson
admin@livingathisfeet.org

FIRST EDITION, 2014

Special discounts are available on quantity purchases by corpo-
rations, associations, and others. Orders by US trade bookstores
and wholesalers. For details, contact the author at the e-mail
address above.

ISBN: 9780984968794
Publisher: Living at His Feet Publications

Editing, cover, & interior design: Inksnatcher.com

DEDICATION

*Firstly, I want to dedicate this book to my husband, Jerame.
He has been my number one supporter in life and ministry; he has
always believed in my dreams, my future, and me; he pushes me to
reach my greatest potential; and he pulls the gold out of me. I thank
God for him.*

*Secondly, I dedicate this book to my parents, who have
been great supporters in my life and in my journey with the Lord
throughout my life. They have given me their blessing in every move
the Holy Spirit told me to make, even when it didn't make sense to
the natural mind. Because of them I have learned to give generously,
love graciously, and take responsibility. They are an inspiration to
many, including me.*

CONTENTS

Introduction

About the Author

❈ INTRODUCTION ❈

Are you ready to step up to the plate, overcome your fears, be bold and courageous, and begin to walk in your God-given authority on the earth? Are you ready for the impartation of your life? Are you ready to be blown away with how God will use you?

If you answered yes to these questions, then I dare you to read on and receive an impartation as you read the stories and glean from the Scriptures. You, too, can begin to walk in the supernatural power and authority of Christ as a son or daughter of the King! Through the pages of this book, I hope to communicate a message of hope and excitement regarding that which is available to us as children of God. So sit back, read, and receive!

— Miranda

1

IT'S AN ADVENTURE

It had been a bright sunny day—perfect for a hike, perfect for a mountain climb. I was living in Brisbane, Australia, at the time, in transition between missions and simply living, working, and growing in the Lord. My closest friends at the time—ones that I had so quickly grown to love, trust, and share my heart with—were also ones who enjoyed the same level of adventure and risk that I carried, and more. On this particular afternoon my friend, her family, and I decided to rock climb to the top of one of the beautiful mountains in the state of Queensland, Australia. After driving about an hour, full of excitement and joy, we arrived at the mountain ready to start our day's adventure.

I'll never forget that day. So much transpired and I learned so much on that little adventure. I leaped over fear, discovered my authority, and grew in my personal faith. It was a day of the unknown, a day that carried potential disaster, and a day that was filled with the goodness of God. So we set out. Gripping rocks, sticking our toes in the clefts of rocks, and pulling ourselves up onto ledges was a bit of what we endured during our climb. At times we challenged ourselves to step off the beaten path and make our own route.

It was during one of those moments when I truly had to face my fear. My two friends were fearless and challenged me in many ways—good ways. They were fearless for the Lord, full of faith and courage, and one of them jumped high onto the cliff ahead of me like a mountain goat would step up onto a steep rock ledge. I stared up at him and wondered how on earth I was going to get up there. To me, it seemed to be a tall, steep, and intimidating cliff wall. My brave female friend hadn't yet jumped up, but noting my intimidation, she offered to stand below me and catch me if I fell. She was notably petite, but for some reason her bravery and offer to stand below me gave me the boost of courage that I needed. I gripped the rock ledge and awkwardly pulled myself up, using all my strength. As I reached the top, the words that came out of my friend's mouth hugely encouraged me. She told me that the Holy Spirit had spoken to her when she offered to catch me if I fell. He had told her, *Do you really think that you're going to be able to catch Miranda?* Then He opened her eyes to a massive angel that stood directly behind me, giving her the faith that heaven offered much greater help and would not let God's children fall to the ground.

I was reminded of the Scripture in Psalm 91:1-4, "He who dwells in the shelter of the Most High will abide in the shadow of the Almighty. I will say to the Lord, 'My refuge and my fortress, my God, in whom I trust!' For it is He who delivers you from the snare of the trapper and from the deadly pestilence. He will cover you with His pinions, and under His wings you may seek refuge; His faithfulness is a shield and bulwark." Trust is one of the biggest things in life … trusting God, trusting people, trusting. Although people may let us down, God never does, and trusting God and my friends in this particular experience was key. Neither let me down.

I was so encouraged by this experience, because I realized that when God calls us to do something—no matter how intimidating or fearful the task might be—He *always* provides a way out and the protection and courage that we need to conquer. Gideon had an experience like this. He was of the least of the clans of Israel, and yet an angel of the Lord visited him and called him a mighty warrior (see Judges 6:12). The Lord called

Gideon to lead an army and even to take dominion in places where it seemed absolutely impossible (i.e. the 300 versus the innumerable number of enemy soldiers mentioned in Judges 7: 2-8). God is always testing our faith in order to demonstrate His authority and faithfulness.

Rain!

As my friends and I climbed a little higher and finally made it to the top, we stopped, breathed, and took in the remarkable view. As we did, however, what we saw surprised us—thick rain clouds started moving in very quickly on us. Raindrops began to sprinkle on our heads and the mountains slowly darkened due to the overshadowing of the clouds. Panic could have easily settled in; we all realized what this meant. With the steep rocks beneath us and rains coming in to wet their surfaces, the ground would become too slippery to make it back down safely.

It was time we stepped into the authority Jesus commissioned us with. It was time we used the power of our tongues to take ownership of the situation. My girlfriend, full of faith and confidence, stepped up to the plate and informed our guy friend and myself that Jesus had already given us total authority to take dominion in a situation like this, and that it was our mandate to speak to the rain clouds. She said confidently,

"God wouldn't have allowed us to get all the way up here if He wasn't also going to let us get down."
We both agreed.

She said, "Let's agree on a direction to send the clouds in, and then all three of us will command the clouds to go in that direction."

So the three of us all agreed to send the clouds back in the direction they were coming from. On the count of three we pointed at the clouds, which were still moving in rapidly and further darkening the sky, and spoke audibly and in unison to

God's creation:

"In the name of Jesus, we command you, rain clouds, go *back* in the direction you started from!"

At that very moment, the clouds stopped in their tracks; we watched as they notably switched direction and reversed course. Suddenly the skies cleared and lit up again with the brilliant sunshine we'd climbed in, every little raindrop stopped, and we were able to descend the mountain onto dry ground!

I learned a major lesson that day—I learned that God has given us complete authority and *it's our job to use it.* There's power in the tongue and there's an authority that every saint has been given. It's our job to walk in it, that we might see His kingdom come and His name glorified! After the eye-opening experience that I had that day in Australia, the Lord set me on a journey of discovery and growth in walking in my God-given authority: I began to walk in a whole new realm of faith and I began to step out in confidence as a daughter of the King in a way that I hadn't before.

PRAYER

God, I want to live *your* adventure. I want to start out on this journey of discovering my authority in Christ through daily circumstances. Help me gain confidence and know who I am as a child of God, so that I might quickly stand up to the lies before me. Help me overcome my fears and understand and believe in the help of heaven. Help me take ownership of the different situations that come my way and stand in the authority you've given me; in Jesus's name, amen.

THOUGHTS/NOTES/REVELATION

THOUGHTS/NOTES/REVELATION

2.

🎇 FOREVER CHANGED 🎇

Pushing away anxiety and braving up to the task has been the story of my life. In fact, I've changed so much since my high school days that when I had the privilege, years later, of going back to my conservative Christian high school and speaking in the chapel services one day, the principal—a former teacher of mine—barely recognized me! He was looking around for a shy girl, and I blew him out of the water when I got up and began to speak with charisma, passion, and life. So much had changed in me that the authority of God began to manifest in those services, and when I released a decree at the end of the meetings for the kingdom of heaven to invade that place, students began to rush down to the platform, some with tears in their eyes.

None of those kids knew that Jesus had the power to heal or speak into their lives that day, but when the decree came forth by the authority I've been given in Christ, many were healed! Basketball players who hadn't been able to play in months, because of ankle and wrist problems, were running to the gym to test out their joints and discovering that all pain had left them! They were running back down to the platform to testify of the goodness of God. Others were healed of broken elbows and such. I, along with my friend (whom I had brought with me for support), began to prophesy and speak words of knowledge and destiny into individuals' lives, and the kids were blown away with how God knew them. This is the authority of

Christ, and this is the power of transformation. Teachers saw me in a different light because I was no longer the insecure little girl that I was in high school.

I think there are a lot of us out there who need this—a boldness and courage to push past fear and overcome as faith-filled, courageous warriors for Christ. The Holy Spirit transforms us. We need the Holy Spirit to fill us, change us, and anoint us. Boldness and faith comes by the power of the Holy Spirit. This is what happened for me, and this is what He wants to do for you!

> *For God has not given us a spirit of timidity, but of power and love and discipline* (II Timothy 1:7).

When I was first baptized in the Holy Spirit, I was forever changed. I went from being that shy, timid, fearful girl who was intimidated by people to becoming bold and radical for Jesus. In fact, I became unstoppable in the eyes of many, sharing the good news of Jesus with people everywhere—both in word and power! God wants to transform you so that you walk in absolute faith and boldness, moving out in the authority Jesus commissioned you with. He called you to "go into all the world and preach the gospel to all creation" (Mark 16:15). Jesus also said, "These signs will accompany those who have believed: in my name they will cast out demons, they will speak with new tongues; they will pick up serpents, and if they drink any deadly poison, it will not hurt them; they will lay hands on the sick, and they will recover" (Mark 16:17-18).

We are called to live in faith and not fear, to be a witness wherever we go. The Holy Spirit transformed me and the Holy Spirit wants to transform you. Even Peter, a disciple of Jesus and called to be "the rock on which the church would be built" (Matt. 16:18), was afraid, and he lacked faith to the point of denying Christ before the crucifixion … but after the Holy

Spirit fell on the day of Pentecost, he was forever changed. He began to preach the gospel with boldness, and thousands were saved because of his bold preaching. Acts 1:8 says ". . . but you will receive power when the Holy Spirit has come upon you; and you shall be my witnesses both in Jerusalem, and in all Judea and Samaria, and even to the remotest part of the earth." The way to transformation is through the Holy Spirit. The way to boldness is by the Spirit of God. If we are going to become successful witnesses on the earth, then we need to be forever changed by the power of the Holy Spirit.

Looking to others

For too long the people of God have looked to the ministers of God to perform His great and mighty works. Instead of the body of Christ doing what the body of Christ is called to do, it has left all the work for the mouthpieces/ministers. It's time the body of Christ began to step into all that she's called to do so that Jesus can come back for His warrior bride, all of us equipped and marching forth with confidence in our calling. Jesus is the most humble king you will ever meet. He is so humble that He said to the disciples, "You will do these works and greater because I go to My Father" (John 14:12). It's important to see that Jesus, our humble elder brother, has a longing in His heart to see His followers—his brothers and sisters—do even greater works than He did. That means it's time we took a risk. It's time we stepped out in faith and learned to walk in the authority and calling God has placed upon us.

All authority

I awoke in my Korean hotel room one morning, several years ago, to the Lord saying over and over and over again to me: "All authority in heaven and on earth has been given to me...." That one phrase from Matthew 28:18 also ran through my head during the entire dream. All night I had been dreaming about the authority that God wanted to release on his people. I was about to preach one of my first full revival services ever, and I had woken up with the insight of what I was to release to that group of approximately 2500 hungry Koreans. The Lord continuously told me through the night that the people of God needed to know the authority he'd given to them as sons and daughters of God. He told me it was time for the body of Christ to begin to walk out her authority with radical faith and boldness. I was excited about what God wanted to do and about the impartation he was about to release to his sons and daughters! In spite of the excitement, and the confidence that I'd heard the Lord regarding what to preach, I didn't quite know what I had in me; up 'til that point I hadn't had a lot of experience in running entire conference sessions. It was a total situation of trust in which I had to push away any fear or anxiety and simply give myself over to the Holy Spirit.

As I got up to minister that day, I was amazed at what came out of me. I began to see the Holy Spirit at work as I opened my mouth to speak His Word, and the Word of God began to flow through me freely. Scripture by Scripture and testimony after testimony, Jesus began to reveal His heart and His desire to empower the people. Revelation poured out upon the saints, and their eyes began to be opened to the power and authority they'd been commissioned with. By the end of the message, people were running to the altar to give their hearts to Jesus; souls were being saved and the saints were being activated, all because of a message on empowerment and authority. In fact, we came back to that same church four months later, and no longer were there no miracles or power manifest in that church. Not only had the senior leaders begun to see miracles through their hands, the regular churchgoers were also seeing healing miracles take place out on the streets! That church and those people were *forever changed*!

It's time to rise up in our God-given authority and walk

as the believers that God has called us to be. When people understand that it's in Jesus that true power is demonstrated, they want it. When authority is demonstrated, salvation comes easily. The Lord Jesus is the greatest power and greatest authority there is. No other god has both the *love* and *power* that God Almighty has. Buddhists come running when they see that Jesus heals the sick; Muslims come running when they see that our God demonstrates real love through power; cults repent when the Spirit of Truth is revealed. Jesus is out to reveal His heart, His reality, and His love, and it's time we step in as coheirs with Christ to perform His works and see His kingdom come on earth!

PRAYER

Lord, I want to be changed for your glory. Fill me with your Spirit and fill me with boldness. Get rid of any bit of timidity inside me and make me radical for you! I invite you, Holy Spirit, to come in and transform me!

THOUGHTS /NOTES /REVELATION

3.

❧ BORN FOR PURPOSE ❧

That morning in South Korea, when all that kept ringing through my head as I awoke was: "All authority …," I knew that the Holy Spirit was trying to talk to me about Jesus's commission (in Matthew 28:18-20) to His disciples before He was about to ascend into heaven to take His seat at the right hand of the Father: "All authority has been given to Me in heaven and on earth. Go therefore and make disciples of all the nations, baptizing them in the name of the Father and the Son and the Holy Spirit, teaching them to observe all that I commanded you; and lo, I am with you always, even to the end of the age." This is what we call the Great Commission.

At that point in my life, I'd already been operating in the miraculous and the authority of Christ on the streets and in the marketplace; I'd already seen many incredible things by the grace and authority of the Holy Spirit, but it was at this point—the start of my international ministry—when I realized what God wanted. His desire is to ingrain in the hearts and minds of believers, all around the world, the depth of supernatural power that lies within the saints. In a time and day when "darkness covers the earth and the people" (Is. 60:1), it is vital that we know the authority we've been given in Christ.

Identity
First things first: we need to know our identity as sons and daughters of God. The Bible teaches us that God is our Father

and we are His children. If the Bible is true, and I believe that it is, then that means we have an inheritance that comes directly from the throne room of the King. What is that inheritance? It's the promise of adoption! Ephesians 1:5 says "He predestined us to adoption as sons through Jesus Christ to himself, according to the kind intention of His will." We are sons! [That goes for the ladies as well … we are daughters of the Father of our Lord Jesus Christ. I simply say sons because there is no gender in God; all are "sons," just as both men and women are to become the bride of Christ. Paul writes in Galatians 3:28: "There is neither Jew nor Greek, there is neither slave nor free man, there is neither male nor female; for you are all one in Christ Jesus."]

As sons of God we have nothing to fear, nothing to hide. We can have this confidence, because as God's children, we are His pleasure and His prized possession. People are imperfect, and even the best fathers and mothers make mistakes in raising their children, but God is *the* perfect father and His heart is *for* us, not against us. Even the best fathers here on the earth cannot match the perfection and love of our heavenly father. His desire is for us. He longs to see His children excel in all that they put their hands to.

We sometimes miss out on all that God has for us because oftentimes, when we get saved, we give our hearts to God and love Him, but we have a wrong understanding of who He is and what we are here on earth for. Oftentimes we take our childhood experiences and apply them to our understanding of who God is. That's wrong. We need to stand on the Word of God and believe who He says we are and who the Scriptures say He is.

-God is good.
-He's perfect in every way.
-He desires to give us every good and perfect gift.
-He's given us relationship.

-He's given us forgiveness, even when we didn't deserve it.

-He's given us *love*.

With that love comes trust, and He trusts us with the same authority He entrusted to Jesus when Jesus walked the earth. That's a high calling. That's the power of sonship.

Purpose

Too often we run around wondering what to do with our lives. Every day people are abusing their bodies, doing senseless things, walking in depression, and having no goals or purpose for their lives. As children of God and heirs to His kingdom, we have purpose! We have destiny! You have been called *for such a time as this* to release God's authority and see His plans fulfilled here on the earth! God has chosen you to co-labor with Him in reaching a lost and dying world.

In whatever is in your heart to do, do it with passion. Whether you go to school, work in a supermarket, are a stay-at-home mom, work as a businessman, or if you're called to be a full-time minister—whatever you do, have in mind the heart of the kingdom! Whatever you do, know that you're called to release the power of the Holy Spirit in that place. This is your ultimate purpose; this is your ultimate destiny. You have been called to change society, to affect the lives of those you come across, and it's all through knowing who you are in Christ: a coheir. Our mandate on the earth is to accomplish the will of the Father—to love God and love people and make Him known.

I started out in Youth With a Mission—a worldwide missions organization whose mission statement is that we would "know God and make Him known." This, I believe, is the mission statement of the Father. How can we walk out our God-given authority if we first do not know who our Father is? We must get into the place of intimacy with the Father, knowing the heartbeat of Jesus and walking as one with the Holy

Spirit, so that we can then walk in the true authority of Christ and release His love and power on the earth! Jesus commissioned the disciples in John 9:4, saying: "We must work the works of Him who sent [Jesus] as long as it is day." This is our purpose—to know God, know that we are sons, and then walk out in the authority that we've been given!

In the letter to the Ephesians, Paul writes:

> *Blessed be the God and Father of our Lord Jesus Christ, who has blessed us with every spiritual blessing in the heavenly places in Christ, just as He chose us in Him before the foundation of the world, that we would be holy and blameless before Him. In love He* **predestined us to adoption as sons** *through Jesus Christ to himself, according to the kind intention of His will, to the praise of the glory of His grace, which He freely bestowed on us in the Beloved* (Eph. 1:3—7; emphasis mine).

From the beginning of time, God the Father *destined* you and me to be His kids! "He is good, for His lovingkindness is everlasting" (Psalm 136:1)! Not only that, "He made known to us the mystery of His will" (Eph. 1:9), and "we have obtained an inheritance, having been predestined according to His purpose who works all things after the counsel of His will" (Eph. 1:11).

Destiny

I want to look at a story in the Bible that paints a perfect picture of where we stand as sons of God and as beacons of light. You will see the purpose-filled destiny of a young lady who was once an unseen orphan child but she blossomed into a beautiful queen. She was—you could say—predestined from the beginning of time, by God, to save a nation! She was born for a purpose, born to walk out a God-given authority, but it all started with her identity. In an era many years ago—long before

Jesus walked as the Son of Man on the earth, this woman had to overcome fear to bring a nation from an impossible situation into a glorious and bright future....

In a time when the Israelites were living under the ungodly kingship of King Ahasuerus, after having come in exile years before by King Nebuchadnezzar, there was a young Jewish orphan girl named Hadassah (also called Esther). This young lady lost both of her parents as a little child and, as a result, her cousin Mordecai took Esther into his care—out of her place of abandonment—and adopted her into his family. This former orphan girl was graced by God and predestined with a glorious future.

Esther was chosen by the king's men to come before the (ungodly) king Ahasuerus as one who would potentially replace Queen Vashti. Esther had beauty and grace going for her, but more than anything, she had the *favor* and *destiny* of God on her life. She went through twelve months of preparation before she came before the king. After the beautification process was complete, she was bathed in oils and fragrances and brought before the king, where she found favor in his sight. She quickly became queen—transitioning from being just an *unseen orphan* girl to *queen*! No one in the king's quarters knew Esther's Jewish roots, but God had a **purpose** in her being there—a major purpose.

While Esther reigned with the king in his kingdom, Mordecai continued to check up on his cousin every day and make sure she was doing well. At the same time, Haman—King Ahasuerus's right-hand man—became angry with Mordecai because he would not bow down to Haman. As a result, Haman plotted to kill Mordecai, and eventually it turned into a plot for the annihilation of all the Jews. However, what looked like a desperate situation became a prime opportunity for a child of God, a prime opportunity to use the authority and position God had put her in for that situation. [There are plenty

of desperate situations on the earth today, and rather than looking through eyes of fear, it's our job to look with God's eyes—
eyes of faith, eyes of hope, eyes of potential. We have the ability
to see the situation as an *opportunity* to display God's glory and
authority to the world, rather than run from it in fear.

When Mordecai learned of Haman's plot, he called for
Esther through a servant, brought the plot to her attention, and
uttered these key words (which are key for us today): "Who
knows whether you have not attained royalty for such a time as
this?" (Esther 4:14). You see, Mordecai had the revelation that
it was not simply because of natural circumstances that Hadassah (Esther) became queen; it was because of the perfect plans
of the Lord. Mordecai understood that Esther was not in the
position of authority she was in merely to look pretty and enjoy
life; she was there for a purpose. She was there because God
had ordained her to be there—adopted and chosen and destined to make a difference. Mordecai put a challenge before her
to step out of her comfort zone, approach the king, and use her
authority as queen to take a stand for righteousness.

Just like Esther, you have been placed on the earth for
such a time as this. You are called to change the scope of history! It is not by accident that you are here; it is for a purpose.
God has plans to use you, even amid a dark time and dark
people. Just like Mordecai challenged Esther, the Holy Spirit
is challenging *you*. He's putting a challenge out that we would
use the authority we've been given in the kingdom and step
out in boldness for the sake of righteousness, for the sake of
rescuing people out of a place of spiritual bondage and death.
We must come to understand the revelation that He wants to
use us as lights in a dark world and that he wants us to respond
to darkness with faith and boldness. The Bible says in Romans
8:15-17 that "you have not received a spirit of slavery leading
to fear again, but you have received a spirit of adoption as sons
by which we cry out, 'Abba! Father!' The Spirit himself testi-

fies with our spirit that we are children of God, and if children, heirs also, heirs of God and fellow heirs with Christ ..." This Scripture demonstrates that boldness comes with the revelation of being called sons. "You have not received a spirit [...] leading to fear," rather, you are coheirs with Christ and sons of God. It's time we step out of our orphan mentalities and step into *sonship*. Kingdom authority is part of our *inheritance*. If we're going to walk in that kingdom authority, we must understand that we are children of God and that we have been born for *purpose*.

PRAYER

Lord, thank you that you have chosen me for such a time as this. Thank you that you have placed me on the earth for a specific purpose: to shine your light and reveal your love to people. Thank you that you've called me your child. Help me to walk in the revelation that I am a child of God, and that as your child I have been given authority on the earth to release heaven. Help me to walk in this authority. Teach me what it means to walk out the authority you've given to me. In Jesus's name, amen.

THOUGHTS/NOTES/REVELATION

4.

🐾 WORDS WITH WEIGHT 🐾

So now that we know we are born into the family of God and are coheirs with Christ, called as sons and daughters of God and born for purpose, what does it mean to walk out that authority? What does it look like to carry out the authority of God? Second Corinthians 5:20 says that we are "ambassadors for Christ, as though God were making an appeal through us." An ambassador is someone who is sent with the same authority as the one who sent him. Jesus said in the Great Commission: "All authority has been given to Me in heaven and on earth. Go therefore …" (Matt 28:18—19). You see, Jesus sent us, His disciples, with *all* of the authority that He had been given. That authority contains the power to speak a word and see it established. When (on earth) a king or queen speaks forth a decree, it is done. When Jesus—King of Kings— speaks forth a word, it is absolutely done.

In the beginning of time, the Holy Spirit hovered over the earth and God breathed into that realm of the Spirit; He spoke a word and light happened (see Genesis 1:1-3). Now that the Spirit of God dwells in *you* (and Jesus has commissioned you with the same authority that He possesses), when you speak a word by the Spirit of God, that word creates something. There is power in the tongue, power in the words you speak. Proverbs 18:21 says "Death and life are in the power of the tongue, and those who love it will eat its fruit." With the authority of Christ, your words specifically carry weight. That weight is authority.

> *Your words have power to create life and*
> *they have power to produce death.*

      It's important that we are aware of what we're declaring over a person, place, or even over ourselves, because those words actually do contain power. James 3:8-10 says "But no one can tame the tongue; it is a restless evil and full of deadly poison. With it we bless our Lord and Father, and with it we curse men, who have been made in the likeness of God; from the same mouth come both blessing and cursing." It is vital that we know what we are doing when we speak forth a word—we are releasing authoritative words, words that can create, words that can bring death. We must speak forth the words of Christ and the words of life. When we speak forth life, life happens. When we speak forth creativity, creation happens.

      In the story of the centurion soldier in Luke 7, he sent Jewish elders to approach Jesus and tell Him that his slave was ill at home and about to die. While Jesus was on His way to the centurion soldier's house, the soldier sent out friends to tell Jesus that he was not worthy for the Lord to come to his home, and that all he needed was for Jesus to "*say the word* and [his] servant would be healed" (Luke 7:7). Jesus went on to commend the man for his great faith and, of course, He spoke the word and the servant was later found at home completely restored and in good health (Luke 7:10). You see, the soldier understood authority. He was a man in authority and he understood the weight of his words on those he was in authority over, so he also knew that Jesus—walking in God, given authority on the earth—could simply speak the word and his servant would be healed. We need faith like this. We have been commissioned with the same authority as the One who sent us (see 2 Cor. 5:20) and, therefore, we have the same authority as Jesus had to be able to speak a word and see it established (see Job 22:28).

Good words create life
Have you ever dropped a weight on your foot? Or maybe you've picked one up in an incorrect manner, resulting in a pulled tendon or nerve. This can be likened to the power of a negative word on a person. Weights are meant to *build up*, not to injure. If used correctly, they are a powerful tool in strengthening the physical body and providing definition to the muscles. When weights are used wrongly, though, or in the case I mentioned—you accidently drop a free weight on yourself—they *hurt*! Not only do they hurt, they can easily seriously damage a part of your body when used incorrectly. Weights were never intended to bring destruction; they were intended to produce strength. In the same way, words were never intended to tear down; they were intended to produce *life*! They were not fashioned to kill. Only the thief comes to steal, kill, and destroy. Jesus "came that they may have life, and have it abundantly" (John 10:10). The authority of Christ was never designed to be used in a damaging way; it was intended to procreate with Him for *good*. We are called to produce good fruit. Your words can either produce good fruit or they can kill. I don't know about you, but I want to be one who creates good things by the authority of Jesus.

Creating with words
When I was younger and in a season of learning about the authority our words carry as sons and daughters, I had many situations that taught me the weight of them. One time a roommate was driving me to a meeting. Prior to setting out, she accidently poked herself in the eye ... hard. When she did this her eye immediately reddened, puffed up, closed, and felt very painful to her. She drove me to the meeting while able to see only out of her good eye.

As I was getting out of the car, I simply said to her—almost halfheartedly—, "Be healed." I quickly got out of the car and started into the building where the meeting was. Moments later my friend burst through the front doors and into the building after me, saying that her eye was completely healed! The redness left, the puffiness went down, and the pain completely left! This all happened by a simple word spoken in authority. Life and death is in the power of the tongue. I hadn't prayed with passion or intensity, or even labored over the "miracle"; all I did was state a simple command: "Be healed." This is what it means to walk in God's authority. *Your words carry weight.*

Do you understand that you have the power to create? We are coheirs with Christ, and He has commissioned us with the same authority He has, meaning we have the same power to create by His Spirit! Life and death are in the power of the tongue, and when you speak forth a word of life, *something* happens; therefore, when you speak forth a creative miracle over someone in need of a new limb, *something* happens. When a person has a deaf ear from birth and you come alongside him, pray for him, and speak a word of life over him, creative power is released. You have the power to create and the authority to release the miracle—you have the working power of Jesus! When you speak forth the word of life by the name of Jesus, life happens and that deaf ear should pop open.

The key to releasing the authority of God through our words is faith. So often I hear people pray with desperation and anguish, but in their sincere sympathy for a person, their prayers are almost said in doubt rather than decreed in faith. The difference between an orphan and a son is in his views and upbringing. While an orphan never knows when he will be provided for, and thus is often found begging for bread, a son knows that food will be regularly put before him on the table. The same is true in the kingdom. An orphan mindset will cause you to beg for a miracle, repeating the same prayer over and over again in hopefulness, but with a twinge of doubt and fear that it won't happen. A son of the King who knows who he is will confidently decree the miracle, knowing that his needs are already met. When it comes time for you to step out and pray for a sick person, try making a simple declaration rather than begging with a long doubtful prayer. For example, "I speak to that broken bone and I command it to be made new now. In Jesus's name I command all the pain and the fracture to go!" Something so simple, yet so authoritative, is what will unlock the miracle. This is faith and this is authority.

God's heart

Job 22:28 says "You will also declare a thing, and it will be established for you; so light will shine on your ways." Authority through sonship in the kingdom means that you hear the voice of God, you do what He says to do, and it is done. Authority means that Jesus has your back. When you know God and know who you are in Christ, you begin to know the heart of God. When you know the heart of God, you begin to see things through heaven's perspective and God's desires become your desires. You begin asking for what heaven wants to see done on the earth. Since God is simply looking for His family to partner with Him in seeing heaven come on earth (see Jesus's famous prayer in Matthew 6:10), it is not hard to see heaven manifest on earth through that partnership. God's got your back, and He will back your words to see those things established. As well, when something pertains to getting the gospel of Christ and the gospel of the kingdom of God to the lost and hurting, God sees a special need in backing up His children. Let me share an example with you:

I was living in Redding, California, back in 2005; I was growing in my walk of authority and power and fully walking out a radical boldness for evangelism, healing, and souls. I would regularly go out to the streets, malls, gas stations, and parks to witness, pray for the sick, and expect to see God move. I devoted my Saturdays to bringing food to the skate park as a sign of God's love, and as a way of opening up conversations with not only the skaters in the park, but also the homeless living in the area. On one particular day, I was driving with my friend to the park, but thick clouds and rain were threatening to stop us from going and would, most likely, push the people away. As we were driving my friend said,

"Miranda, why don't you command the clouds to part and the sun to come out?"

Instantly I obeyed with faith like a child, opened the window and commanded, "In the name of Jesus, clouds and rain go away and we call forth the sun!"

As soon as I released the decree, we watched as the clouds parted and the sun began to shine! The rain stopped and it turned out to be a nice sunshiny day! This experience not only illustrates the power of words, but it shows the heart of God. He is simply *looking* for His sons and daughters to begin to walk in their authority and take dominion over situations that might stand in the way of getting His love out! We can no longer let fear hold us back; it's time to take up our authority, listen to the heart of God, and "decree a thing" to see it established (see Job 22:28).

The same Spirit
God created the universe out of nothing. He spoke and light happened. He decreed and creation took place. As sons and daughters of God, adopted in by the redemption of Jesus Christ, that same Spirit that raised Christ Jesus from the dead lives in us. As sons and daughters of God, the same creative Spirit that hovered over the earth (when God spoke life into being) lives in us. We need to begin to speak and declare out of the heart of the King and by the Spirit of God, and creative miracles will begin to take place. The supernatural is available

and should be natural to every believer.

One time in the little country town of Te Aroha, New Zealand, my husband and I were doing healing meetings. God gave me a word of knowledge for someone who had nerve damage and lack of feeling down the left side. A man came forward stating that he had a stroke when he was still in his mother's womb. As a result, he had lack of feeling and mobility all down his left side. He had terrible weakness and lack of mobility in his leg, and his arm and hand were withered. The man couldn't lift his arm, and there was pain if he tried. His hand was bent in from nerve damage, and the man was extremely discouraged, but shocked that God would call him up to touch him.

Creative power comes out of the heart of God, and it manifests through faith like a little child's and a declaration of God's kingdom. I began to decree movement over this man. I began to take authority and decree that strength and mobility would come into the nerves. All of a sudden strength began to fill the man's side. All of a sudden the man's eyes got wide as he realized that he had supernatural strength in his left leg. Then power began to fill his arm, and we watched as his hand sprang out and his arm stretched out with feeling and strength! Tears began to fill this man's eyes as he felt the love of God so strongly. Slowly he began to raise his arms in worship to the Lord … this being the one thing that he had always wanted to do yet never could because he had no feeling in his left arm. For minutes the man stood there in awe and shock at the love and creative power of God!

God is the God of restoration, and He loves to pour out healing power over a hurting, broken world—healing both the physically and emotionally hurting. That man was touched in a powerful way that day. All it took was someone who was willing to step out in faith, be obedient to the still small voice of the Lord highlighting a condition, and the willingness to decree creative power and love into a crippling condition. That man will never be the same. The next day I overheard him testifying to someone how he still couldn't believe that God loved him so much that He would heal his body like that. Powerful.

The creative power of God manifests through the authority we carry in our words! It's time we start using our tongues to bless and not curse. It's time we start using our words to decree life and not death. The Bible says that life and death is in the power of the tongue. James 3 says that with the tongue we bless God with, we also curse people with. It's time we blessed and spoke life over our fellow brothers and sisters!

PRAYER

Lord, I ask that you would help me with my words. Help me understand the power of my words and the weight that is behind words that I speak. Let me use the anointing of creative power and authority that you've destined me to walk with. Let me use my words for your glory, Jesus, that miracles would happen through the words that I speak; in Jesus's name, amen.

THOUGHTS/NOTES/REVELATION

THOUGHTS/NOTES/REVELATION

5.

🎋 POWER VS. AUTHORITY 🎋

With all the false displays of supernatural power out in the world today, it's important to understand that Jesus has the ultimate power. Even more, His power has authority behind it. Sometimes I think people get scared of the miraculous because all they've ever seen has been a demonic demonstration of power. The truth of the matter is that demons do have a form of power, but Jesus has ultimate authority. What's the difference?

1 John 4:4 reads, "You are from God, little children, and have overcome them; because greater is He who is in you than he who is in the world." You don't need to fear the devil because Jesus—the anointed one—is *in* you and He is Lord over all! He defeated death on the cross and took back the keys of hell and Hades. It's silly to be afraid of supernatural power just because there's a dark side out there. All through the Bible there are countless supernatural power encounters demonstrating God working with His people. If we were to throw out supernatural power, we would be throwing out God. God is all-powerful and loves to put His power and glory on display.

You were born for such a time as this, and you were born to host the Spirit of God inside you. This being true, you are called to walk in the power of God and to put to shame the powers of darkness. Ephesians 1:22 says "... He put all things in subjection under His feet, and gave Him as head over all things to the church ..." Everything of darkness is under the feet of Jesus! We don't need to fear the powers of darkness because Jesus crushes them by His authority! Earlier in the same chapter, Paul prays for the Ephesians, and we can take that as a prayer for us today:

"I pray that the eyes of your heart may be enlightened, so that you will know what is the hope of His calling, what are the riches of the glory of His inheritance in the saints, and what is the *surpassing greatness of His power* toward us who believe" (Eph. 1:18-19; emphasis mine).

Paul understood that the saints would struggle with this revelation, but it is crucial in our walk with God to know that we have been *called,* and not only called, but that the greatness of His power is for us who *believe*! Paul the apostle goes on in his prayer for the saints of Ephesus: "… These are in accordance with the working of the strength of His might which He brought about in Christ, when He raised Him from the dead and seated Him at His right hand in the heavenly places, far above all rule and authority and power and dominion, and every name that is named, not only in this age but also in the one to come" (Eph. 1:19-21).

Jesus rules and reigns far above all powers of darkness on the earth *and* in all spiritual realms. The devil may have a form of power, but it is nothing in comparison to the power and authority of Christ!

God's backing
Moses understood what God's authority looked like. When Moses had his encounter with God on the mountain, the Lord taught him how to use His authority—the authority God was backing him up with. Basically, the Lord simply told Moses to do whatever He told him to do, and say whatever He told him to say. Moses was sent before Pharaoh to tell him to let God's people go. When Pharaoh demanded Moses show him a sign, Moses commanded Aaron to throw his staff on the ground, and when he did the staff became a serpent (see Exodus 7:8-13).

All the magicians and sorcerers in Pharaoh's court threw their staffs down, and theirs all became serpents as well. While they all had a *form* of power, only Moses had God's backing, which was proof he was walking not only in God's power, but also in His *authority*. What was the proof of this authority? Aaron's staff then swallowed up the magicians' and sorcerers' staffs.

This is the difference of power and authority: power demonstrates signs and miracles, but authority demands respect. We know that the Holy Spirit releases power on God's people (see Acts 1:8), but Jesus also commissioned us with authority so that we can walk in His power *and* have His backing. Authority is the higher realm. Even demons have a form of power, but they flee at the name of Jesus. Sometimes all it takes is speaking out truth and then watching as God does the rest.

Delivered!

There was a time my husband and I were about to minister in South Korea in a beautiful port city called Busan. The Holy Spirit spoke to me in advance and said that that particular night would be a powerful night of deliverance. Although I don't focus on deliverance in my ministry, sometimes (because of the goodness and authority of Christ) He moves in that way for the purpose of setting the captives free. So that night I preached a word on overcoming darkness and then encouraged the people to worship God. In the presence of worship, I began to make decrees and proclaim freedom over the people. By the simple word of Christ, many were healed and delivered in the presence of God, simply by a word spoken in authority.

Many people came up to testify of what God had just done for them. One woman, small in stature, testified of her freedom and her story was very touching. She was being abused every day by her husband and, because of the abuse, the woman lived in fear, torment, shame, and anxiety. Not only that, she was in physical pain from head to toe. In the presence of God and by the authoritative word of God, the lady was totally set free! All the pain had left her body and there was no more shame or guilt or fear, only joy and hope! The pastors knew this woman and reported that she didn't even *look* the same after this miracle. Previous to the authority of Jesus being released, her face looked downtrodden and depressed; after Jesus released His authority, her face looked hopeful and joy-filled. This is an amazing miracle of freedom for the oppressed.

When we returned to Korea several months later, the pastors reported that the same lady was *still* doing well! Praise God! This is authority. Demons may have power but Jesus has authority. He's commissioned you with that authority to cast out demons and see the oppressed free!

Pizza

On a more practical note (and something that you as a reader can relate to and see happen through your own life, even if you don't have a platform like mine), there have been many times when we have seen the authority of Christ released to set the captive free on a regular day—on the streets, for example. On one occasion Jerame and I were walking and shopping on the downtown streets of Vancouver, Canada. A homeless man stopped us both and said he was hungry and asked us if we would buy him a piece of pizza. Of course we said yes! As we were walking to the pizza shop with the man, we began to converse with him and ask him why he was living on the streets. The man told us how he was schizophrenic and never stopped hearing voices in his head. For several years he hadn't had peace of mind because the voices never silenced themselves. Jerame and I began to testify to the man that Jesus is the author of peace and that He was willing to touch him. We asked him if, once he was finished eating, we could pray for him. The man immediately stopped in his tracks and put his hands out in front of him, ready to receive. He said,

"Not later, pray now!"

This man was in a desperate situation and hungry for a miracle. He was hungry for the words of Christ to set him free. We immediately laid hands on his shoulders and began to call on the name of Jesus and decree his freedom. The man suddenly started freaking out and testifying that he was feeling the electricity of God flow up and down his body—a sign of the presence and power of the Holy Spirit at work. Then all of a sudden, the man began to listen and testify that all the voices had stopped and his mind was clear for the first time in several years! At the name of Jesus the demons that were tormenting this man's mind had to flee. The authority of Christ breaks the chains and sets the oppressed free. This is your mandate—"to proclaim liberty to the captives and freedom to prisoners" (Isaiah 61:1).

It's yours
Jesus longs to fill you with a power from on high. He longs for you to walk in the fullness of your calling as sons and daughters of God, and to carry the authority of Christ with you so that even demons flee. Paul the apostle prayed for the Ephesians, and now I declare over you, "that [God] would grant you, according to the riches of His glory, to be strengthened with power through His Spirit in the inner man ..." (Eph. 3:16). When we're strengthened with this power that the Holy Spirit bestows on us, we can walk in such a way that no power of darkness can stand before us.

Always remember that "He put all things in subjection under His feet, and gave Him as head over all things to the church, which is His body, the fullness of Him who fills all in all" (Eph. 1: 22-23). Every work of darkness is under the feet of Jesus, and you—the sons of God—are His body. Every demonic stronghold is *under* your feet, saints. It's simply a matter of knowing this and living by it, of being submitted to Jesus and not in submission to fear of the devil. All authority belongs to

Jesus and He has commissioned you to carry out that authority, putting the works of darkness in check and standing boldly in faith before Him, knowing that you've been chosen, called, and commissioned. Authority is greater than power and you've been commissioned with both—commissioned with authority and endued with power from heaven.

In Acts 1:8 Jesus says "you will receive *power* when the Holy Spirit has come upon you; and you shall be My witnesses both in Jerusalem, and in all Judea and Samaria, and even to the remotest part of the earth." Throughout the earth, whether it be in your hometown or on the mission field, you need not fear! Allow the Holy Spirit to fill you continually and anoint you with His power so that you see His kingdom come in every place you go—no matter how dark it may seem. God is light and He is in you! 1 John 1:5 says, "God is Light, and in Him there is no darkness at all." You carry that light, and you are a beacon of His light and power wherever you go.

Real authority
Now here's a key, friends: you can't walk in true authority unless you're under real authority. There are too many people running around not wanting to be in relationship with leaders and thus, they become flakey Christians. We need to have people around us to whom we can be accountable and who can speak into our lives if things come up. Even the centurion soldier mentioned earlier understood how authority worked, and that when authority is released, those under authority must obey. A man was healed because of faith in God and revelation on submission and lordship. We need to get our heart in tune with honor, as well as give Jesus true lordship. He deserves to have His way in and through us, and when we give Him place, we will see the impossible made possible!

I've witnessed a person being healed or a miracle released simply by a decree many times. Again, when we give

Jesus place and when we know our authority, nothing is impossible. All the king had to do for Esther's life to be saved, when she approached him, was speak words of authority. In the same way, all we need to do is be in tune with the Holy Spirit and the heart of the Father, and we will simply speak a word and it will be done.

I was in a meeting in Canada once when the Lord spoke to me and said that someone's family member was in the hospital in a coma at that moment. I asked the congregation if that word of knowledge made sense to someone in the room and, sure enough, a young lady raised her hand and said it was her grandmother. In agreement, we made a decree and called forth life over the young lady's grandmother and decreed that she come out of the coma, in the name of Jesus. After that meeting finished, the girl called her father to get a report on her grandmother. Turns out that right about the same time that we made the decree, her grandmother came out of the coma … laughing! That's the power of the decree and that's the power of submitting to authority.

PRAYER

Lord Jesus, thank you for your authority. Thank you that by your Spirit, not only have I been baptized in power, but I've been commissioned with your authority. Help me walk in such a way that your power and authority are demonstrated through me in places even demons flee from and—by your grace—that I would see the captives set free. Help me to hear your voice and to decree life with my words, seeing creative miracles manifest wherever I go. Provide opportunities for me to release this authority. Set people along my path who are in need of a miracle and in need of freedom from oppression. Help me to walk in boldness, using your authority to see demons flee and see your light invade areas of darkness. Help me submit to those in authority over my life, that I would come into greater authority by first being submitted. You are the perfect example of humility, and I want to model that on earth. I want to model what it looks like to be under leadership, and as a result, flourish in power and authority with words. Thank you for your grace for this, Jesus! In your name I pray, amen!

THOUGHTS/NOTES/REVELATION

6.

EVERY NEED MET

Sons and daughters receive everything they need whenever they need it. In the kingdom of God, He gives bread to the hungry, drink to the thirsty, clothes to the naked, love to the unlovely, healing to the hurting, life to the dying, and so much more ... and He gives us the supplies we require to give to those in need. As sons and daughters of the King, we need to take all the supplies He gives us and run with them. Use those supplies! We have received every spiritual blessing and inheritance from our Father (see Eph. 1:3). It is our right as children of God to grab hold of whatever is in heaven. It is our *mandate* to grab hold of it. Your very *purpose* is to get what the earth needs out of *heaven* and pull it down into earth's realm.

We are spiritual beings, and it is our job to pull out of the Spirit realm that which the physical realm needs. If someone needs a new lung, pull a lung out of the heavenly realm! There's no sickness in heaven! If someone needs freedom from depression, pull joy out of the heavenly realm! It is *your* job as a son/daughter of the King to pull it in. We are *in* the world to not be *of* the world, but to *change* the world. I love Romans 8:32: "He who did not spare His own Son, but delivered Him over for us all, how will He not also with Him freely give us all things?" It is God's *desire* to give us good gifts and provide for our every need. In fact, "your Father has chosen gladly to give you the kingdom" (Luke 12:32)! The problem is we often don't know how to access that realm. With the authority you've been given, you have direct access to the blessings of the kingdom.

Freedom from heaven

Recently I heard the testimony of a man I prayed for several years ago in Europe. He was in a pit of darkness, addicted to heroin, and unable to get out. What are we here for? We're here to pull the *light* of God's glory into places of darkness. You are here for a purpose, and that purpose is to release light and to use your kingdom authority. I prayed over the man, decreeing freedom from the addiction and freedom from the temptation to touch the drug again. A year and a half later, I received the testimony that he has been clean ever since! Praise God! The pastors in the region know him and know this to be a legitimate testimony, and we praise God for the man's freedom! He needed freedom; God gave him freedom. There was no need for rehab because Jesus had him covered. The man's freedom was available in heaven, and all he needed was someone with authority to pull that provision for freedom out of heaven. From a hopeless situation to a glorious future, this man is a testimony of God's greatness and of our purpose being fulfilled on the earth—to use our authority to bring people out of the traps of darkness and into God's glorious light!

Just ask

As children of God, we have every right to approach the throne of grace and ask for what we need when we need it. It's known that on the earth orphans beg for food and live in hopes of just getting a tiny piece of bread; they go from meal to meal knowing it might be their last. Children who grow up in a loving family know that food will be provided for them and that there is always enough. If God is the perfect father, full of love and every good thing, then surely there is *always* enough of everything we need—including healing (healing is the children's bread). Ask and it will be given to you, as sons and daughters of the King. Let that truth sink into your heart: Sonship *is* your inheritance. Your needs *are* fulfilled.

Looking back into our story of Esther, Mordecai had relayed the plans of Haman to Esther and told her she must do something about it. Esther, however, had to overcome her fears in approaching the king. God placed her in a dark kingdom so that He could use her to bring salvation to God's people and fulfill their need for restoration and justice. Natural circumstances told Esther that there was no way she could meet this need. The king had not summoned Esther in thirty days, and according to the rules of his kingdom, no person was permitted to come before the king unless he had first summoned him/her, even if it was the queen herself! Again, natural circumstances told Esther that there was *no way* she could save her people. The penalty was *death* for anyone who came before the king without invitation. There was one exception, however … *if* the king extended his scepter toward the one who approached him, it meant he was extending his *authority* and the penalty of death was bypassed. This said, Esther was terrified to enter the king's courts by her initiation. She was, in a way, *asking* for her own death.

How could a girl who seemed to have attained favor from the Lord be placed in such a position of decision that would potentially not only kick her out of her seat of favor, but put her straight to death? She had been made queen against all odds (she was a Jew, a former orphan, and an exiled victim!), and to just throw away that favor by taking a risk? That is not exactly the decision that most people would want to make. *However*, Mordecai's challenge to her (in Esther 4:14) caused her to be bold and courageous and step out of her comfort zone, even to the point of risking death.

A noble heart *will* make a risky decision
in order to *potentially* take the victory.

The willingness to risk

We have nothing to fear. Philippians 4:8 says "… whatever is true, whatever is honorable, whatever is right, whatever is pure, whatever is lovely, whatever is of good repute, if there is any excellence and if anything worthy of praise, dwell on these things […] and the God of peace will be with you." There is no need to fear risk or obstacles. It is our privilege to meditate on that which is pure and noble and then to call those things out of heaven, knowing that the God of *peace* is not only with us, but also wants to grant us the fulfillment of those noble desires. Esther had to think outside of natural circumstances and focus on what is pure and noble, and then believe for the impossible. She needed to trust that the God of peace was with her and had her back. She needed to trust that her very need was provided for. She went ahead and had the Israelites fast for three days, and then poised herself to go before the king.

What are you willing to do for the sake of God's love for people? Are you willing to step out and take risks for Him? Everything you need is before you; everything of heaven is at hand (see Mark 1:15). It takes a *noble* heart to step out of one's comfort zone and reach for what is at hand. There have been times in my life when I was put in a place of risk—even danger—but rather than be afraid, I chose to walk in confidence. I chose peace. It was the authority of God and the comfort of His presence that overrode the fear factor. When you're focused on God and His love, everything of this earth and everything of darkness seems to fade away. God wants to encase you in His love, boldness, and courage so that you walk as champions rather than victims.

It was because of Esther's bravery and willingness to step out and take a risk that she received the offer and willingness of the king to ask for whatever she wished—up to half the kingdom (see Esther 5:3). Whatever she needed or asked for would be granted her because of her place of favor in the kingdom. In the kingdom of God, when your heart is in line with His, you can ask for that which you desire and it will be done. Jesus said to His disciples, "Whatever you ask in My name, that will I do, so that the Father may be glorified in the Son. If you ask Me anything in My name, I will do it" (John 14:13-14). What you need is accessible in your time of need. You have authority and God wants to grant you favor to release His power and works on the earth.

What is it you need? What is it of God's kingdom that you desire to see established on the earth? In the same way that King Ahasuerus extended the scepter of authority and kingship to Esther, Jesus is extending His authority and grace to you. Grace is the supernatural empowerment to do what you could not do on your own. It's the ability to accomplish what you cannot except by the Spirit of God.

Just before Jesus told His disciples that the things they asked for in His name would be done, he said "he who believes in Me, the works that I do, he will do also; and greater works than these he will do …" (John 14:12). There is no need to worry about the power or provisions to accomplish the tasks that you're called to do when Jesus is on your side. You will do so much more than anything that's been recorded in the Gospels of Christ! Jesus himself said it! The provision to grow out a leg is there; the provision to multiply bread is there; the provision to raise the dead is there. You are able by the grace of God to do the impossible.

Full provision
A prophetic friend of mine had a very real encounter with God, and in it he saw a room in heaven full of body parts. This room made provisions for any organ, body part, or limb that was needed on the earth. The Lord showed him that it is up to us to freely access this room of body parts and call forth that which is not *as though it were.* "Faith is the assurance of things hoped

for and the conviction of things not seen" (Hebrews 11:1). It's our job to access the provisions of heaven and bring heaven to earth (see Matt 6:10). The provision for whatever miracle you need is available and at hand…. "The time is fulfilled, and the kingdom of God is at hand" (Mark 1:15). This goes for not only you, but also those you are praying for. If someone is in need of a new bone or new eyes, call these things forth out of heaven! If you come across a person in need of a new lung, the authority of Christ and the provision of heaven is available to you, and it is your mandate to call forth that new lung out of heaven.

When I was in the beginning stages of walking out my authority in Christ, I had a mama and papa who decided to take a friend and me on a little road trip to Las Vegas. Though many people go to the "City of Sin" to gamble, drink, and have a good time, we were going to have a good time in a different way; we were going to release the kingdom of God. For two days my friend and I walked through the city looking for people we could talk to. At one point early on in our getaway, I noticed a young guy, about eighteen years old, wearing a sling on his right arm. I was immediately drawn to him and began to look for a way to reach the guy and help provide for his need.

We finally crossed paths with him and asked him what had happened to his arm. Turns out the boy had taken a bad fall skateboarding and, as a result, had broken his collarbone … so we knew he was in need of a brand new collarbone. The guy was completely discouraged because it had been the start of a summer of fun and adventure, and he thought his summer was ruined because of his injury. Not so! Jesus provides for all of our needs—physical, emotional, mental, and spiritual! We asked the boy if he wanted to be healed and if we could pray for him. He was completely open because he was desperate for a miracle, so we laid a hand on his shoulder and began to call forth a new collarbone in the name of Jesus. Without asking the guy to check it, and before we could even get done praying, the guy began freaking out and moving his arm around in the sling. He'd felt the power of God touch him and the pain left! We encouraged him to take his arm out of the sling and check his mobility. He ripped the sling off and began flailing his arm around in utter amazement! All the pain had left and the guy was totally healed. Not only that, we led him to Jesus right there, because after he'd seen the power of God touch his body, he was instantly ready to receive Jesus as Savior into his life ... every need met!

Let's begin to walk as sons of God and freely access the provisions of heaven that everyone is in need of.

PRAYER

Father, thank you for all the provisions you have ample supply of. Thank you that you freely make all these provisions accessible to your sons and daughters. Help me to confidently access the gifts of your kingdom and bring heaven to earth so that many will be blessed through me by you. By faith I receive of your provision and am so thankful and blessed that you would freely give to me, your child, whatever I need! You are so good! Let me show the world your goodness and the blessings you want to provide for them! Amen.

THOUGHTS/NOTES/REVELATION

7.

JUST BE YOU!

I was a shy and timid girl once, and then the Holy Spirit changed me. That's what he does. I was a caterpillar in hiding, but God transformed me into a beautiful butterfly, unafraid of the world. This is what God wants to do with the rest of His believers: transform them. He wants to take you out of hiding—out of your cocoon—and present the world to you with endless opportunities to release His kingdom on the earth. The sky is the limit! He wants to awaken you with a radical boldness and make you unafraid of the world out there, moved to demonstrate the power of God with authority whenever the opportunity arises.

Boldness

We can never let intimidation rule our lives. I used to be intimidated and fearful … before I was filled with the Holy Spirit I was even afraid to pray out loud in front of other Christians! I went to a Christian high school (and loved it) and had great friends, really good teachers, a wonderful regular chapel service, Bible class, and even a missions-focused class. Even with all of that *and* a desire to honor God and give Him my whole heart, I was still shy and worried about what people thought of me. My missions teacher loved me, the students were my friends, and we even did ministry trips together—becoming closer and closer as a family. Even still, I was afraid to pray out loud in front of them. The problem was, I didn't know who I was in Christ.

I was afraid to let *me* be me. After Holy Spirit filled me (a few months after I graduated high school), my life was changed, and *boldness* and *faith* became my so-called middle names.

I grew up in a very conservative church. I'd always loved Jesus and studied the Bible, but I didn't know the power of the Holy Spirit. I believe that the Lord really protected my faith and me from so much, because many young people who don't see the power of God in the church get bored and rebel. I'd always stayed faithful to the Lord, but I didn't know the power of the Holy Spirit and the reality of the manifold kingdom of God until I was in my late teens. When I first began to grab a hold of the revelation that Jesus—through me—will heal the sick, I began to go out to the malls, supermarkets, gas stations, and wherever I could, simply to find someone who needed a miracle. It wasn't about me, but God honors those who diligently seek Him, and He works through those who move out in faith and obedience. He honored my faithfulness to take the gospel of the kingdom and step out in it. Everywhere I went, I'd see people instantly healed of arthritis, knee joint pains, broken bones, deafness, and so much more. Some would get saved as a result, and others already were saved but had never seen the power of God before.

One woman that a friend and I prayed for had cerebral palsy from birth and, as a result, she had no feeling down her right side; she couldn't feel any sensation of touch and she was almost completely blind. She could see light and that was about it; she had a dislocated elbow, a dislocated hip, and a kneecap that was flipped upside-down, with tremendous pain as a result. We simply told the lady, after we'd asked her what happened to her and why she had a walker, that we saw miracles and asked if we could pray for her. She was a believer and immediately said yes. As we laid hands on her shoulder and decreed healing, she described a tingling sensation going down her right side—the side that had no feeling before! All of a sudden she began to realize that she could feel us touching her!

As we prayed for her eyesight, first she began to see the frame of my body, then the second time we prayed she began to see the features on my face, and after a third time of praying for her eyes, she looked into the distance and was able to clearly read a sign far off! Out of her own lips, she said,

"I can see 20/20!"

Then we began to pray for her elbow and, sure enough, the pain and lack of mobility left and she could move it freely. We prayed for her hip and her knee, the pain left, and we felt—and she felt—her knee *pop* as if it flipped around the right way! To test out her miracle, we instructed her to try running. The lady responded with a bit of hesitation because she'd never run before, but she agreed to give it a go if we'd run with her. As we linked arms with her, she began to run for the first time in her life! Wow! That's the goodness of God! And see, that's the authority we have as believers ... *heal the sick!*

Great authority

No matter what people may have said about you or what you've even thought about yourself, believe God's truth about you: you're loved, accepted, and a child of God. Because of this, you can walk confidently. David (in the Bible) was a young boy who wasn't moved by what others thought about him; he was moved by what he knew about God. Even though he was the youngest amongst his brothers, and the one that was totally forgotten about when Samuel came to commission the future king, he never let rejection get the best of him. He walked in boldness because God was on his side.

When his brothers all went to the battlefield to fight the Philistines, David was left tending his father's flocks of sheep. As David was faithful with the little and, most importantly, faithful to loving God, God trusted him with much greater responsibilities. Though he was a young guy, when he was sent to check on his brothers in the army and bring food and supplies to them, David was shocked to find that all of the Israelites were hiding in fear. David knew who his God was and operated in the opposite spirit—the spirit of boldness. He approached King Saul and announced that he would fight the giant Philistine called Goliath, since no one else would. Saul tried everything in his power to protect the boy, but God had other plans. We can see here that God chooses those we would least expect to carry the greatest authority and have some of the biggest victories/accomplish some of the greatest feats in life.

> *"But God has chosen the foolish things of the world to shame the wise, and God has chosen the weak things of the world to shame the things which are strong, and the base things of the world and the despised God has chosen, the things that are not, so that He may nullify the things that are, so that no man may boast before God [. . .] so that, just as it is written, "Let Him who boasts, boast in the Lord"* (1 Cor. 1:27—31).

David tried on Saul's armor, but it was all too big on him. He tried walking around in it, but it was uncomfortable and clunky. Instead of trying to fit another man's clothing, David chose to go as he was: protected by the Lord, holding only a slingshot and some rocks from the river brook, along with his shepherd's staff. That staff represented his strength, his authority.

Walk in your God-given authority and walk as God has created you to be; don't try and be something or somebody that you're not. There are times when people may try to put their dreams and visions upon you. Don't let other peoples' hopes and lives rule yours. Allow God to mold you into the person He's called *you* to be. David couldn't fit in Saul's armor, and you can't fit into the armor of people around you. Be the person God has called you to be, and find the strengths and abilities that He's placed in you. This is where you'll have the power to overcome; this is where you'll shine the brightest, and this is where you'll take the victory and see God move on your behalf.

David went out into the battlefield just as he was. Goliath tried mocking him, intimidating him, and threatening him. Nothing Goliath could say stuck to David. David knew what God said about him, and to him that's all that mattered. Goliath began to mock David. He spoke to him saying, "Am I a dog, that you come to me with sticks?" (1 Samuel 17:43). He even cursed David with his gods! None of this threatened or intimidated the young faith-filled shepherd boy, nor did any of those threats affect or stop David, who responded by saying, "You come to me with a sword, with a spear, and with a javelin. But I come to you in the name of the Lord of hosts [...] this day the Lord will deliver you up into my hands." (1 Sam. 17:45-46). This proves boldness; this proves faith. David knew his authority and he knew who his God was. We all know the end of the story: David took out Goliath with just a small stone and then cut off Goliath's head after the giant fell to the ground.

We're positioned
God's called you to take out strongholds, and you can do it by simply knowing who you are and the authority you carry, and by walking in faith and boldness alongside the Holy Spirit. Nothing can take you down when you understand that when God is with you and for you, no one can be against you.

- A key found in David's story is the shepherd's staff—it represents authority. David knew his authority and his position as he approached the giant. It's our mandate to know our authority and know that we're positioned as sons and daughters of the Most High, carrying the strength and authority of Christ.

- David also carried five small stones from the riverbed. Jesus is the chief cornerstone (Ps 118:22; Matt 21:42; Mark 12:10), and we need to walk with Him knowing that He is always at hand, knowing He is with us.

- The riverbed represents the Holy Spirit—being filled up with the Holy Spirit ("Out of your innermost being will flow *rivers* of living water" (John 7:38, emphasis mine)).

- So the key to taking authority over situations in your life, and taking out giants in the land, is walking as you are—in your own gifts and talents and strengths and abilities—and walking in your God-given authority, carrying Christ the Rock everywhere you go, and being continually filled with the Holy Spirit (see Ephesians 5:18).

One time I was just being me as I walked into a sandwich shop with a few friends and, just being me, was overflowing with the joy of the River of Life. As a result, the people working behind the counter wanted to know why I had so much joy and what it was about me that was different. Because I always carry the Rock of Christ with no walls up, that's just who I am, I was able to witness and share the gospel with them! Two people ended up giving their hearts to Jesus that day!

We need to not be afraid of being genuine. The world is looking for real and authentic people. Stop trying to play another person's role and play your own. Get comfortable in your own skin! God created you to be unique, full of all that it takes to have victory in your life and to accomplish great and mighty feats for Him. Sometimes it takes courage to step out in your own skin, but that's where the victory lies; that's when the authority of Christ comes and backs you up! Daniel 11:32 reads: "... but the people who know their God will display strength and take action." When you know who you are and you know who Christ is in you, you won't be afraid to step out *as you are* and see God's kingdom manifest through your life. You will truly see the power of God demonstrated through you when you know who you are and what you carry, and when you walk just as you are, not trying to be somebody that you're not.

Step out

Esther courageously stepped into the king's courts. I can imagine she might have had trembling knees, but she chose to put her trust in God even though her life was on the line. Sometimes it takes laying our own fears aside for the sake of fulfilling a purpose and being used by God. It's in our toughest situations that God makes himself strong. He loves to show himself strong when we are weak. He loves to make possible the impossible when we obey Him.

Sometimes this means stepping out of our "boat" of comfort. The only way Peter was able to walk on water (in Matthew 14:25-31) was by taking a risk and listening to the voice of the Lord. The moment he listened to the voice of Jesus and was obedient, he began to do the impossible. The moment he let his surroundings and the natural circumstances get to his thoughts, the miraculous was put to an end and he began to sink. It's time to put natural circumstances aside and look to the supernatural. Look to Jesus. He goes outside the natural realm. He loves to see impossible situations become possible.

Of course Esther was afraid to approach the king, knowing the potential consequences of her risk, but she chose to live in *faith* instead of *fear*. She put her faith in God, not the natural realm. And we know the outcome: she found favor in the sight of the king. He extended his scepter toward her and said these words: "… what is your request [Queen Esther]? Even to half of the kingdom it shall be given to you" (Esther 5:3). Risk equals blessing! The more we step out in faithfulness to the Lord, the more we see the fruit and blessing of our inheritance in heavenly riches! *Every* spiritual blessing in heavenly places is ours (see Eph. 1:3)!

To finish up the story, let me just remind you that Esther prepared a banquet for the king and for Haman, and then followed it up with a second banquet. Finally at the second banquet, Esther presented her request to the king. She finally informed the king of her people group and spoiled Haman's plan to blot out all of the Jews. When the king found this out, he turned things completely on the "enemy" and issued a decree for the death of Haman and for the life of the Jews. Esther became the hero of the day! She was just an orphan girl! An orphan girl saved the day? This orphan girl had destiny. In the same way, we have destiny! You have the potential and ability to change the course of history and help save a nation!

Our rod of authority

Let us grab hold of something from this wonderful story. It's time we get over our orphan mindsets and come into a revelation of our royalty. We can't keep holding on to our past and being ashamed of what was … it's time to look into the face of the future, into the face of Christ, and embrace His destiny for our lives. The Bible says that we are a royal priesthood. We are no longer fatherless, but we have the most perfect Father of all; He *is* love. No matter what has happened to us in our past, God is able to take it and use it for His glory. He wants to take us from a place of insecurity to a place of confidence in Him—our Father. Esther once was an orphan girl, but she became royalty. We, too, were once orphans, but by the grace of God we are now sons/daughters!

Jesus commissioned us as "ambassadors for Christ" (2 Cor. 5:20). As ambassadors, we're sent with the same authority as the one who sent us. Jesus is asking you the same question King Ahasuerus asked Esther: "What is your request? God is waiting for His royal priesthood to arise with requests of justice to cover injustices. We need to step up and boldly come before the King. How do you know that you weren't brought onto the earth at this time in order to save a nation? Anything is possible for those who believe. This is what the angel Gabriel told Mary at the announcement of Mary's conception in Luke 1:37, and this is what the Word of God is telling you.

I have come across many "impossible" situations over the course of my ministerial years, and regardless of how difficult the situation seemed in fleshly eyes, I have seen God perform the miraculous time and again. It's all about faith, authority, and love. These ingredients produce the miraculous. And it's all about allowing the Holy Spirit to move through *you*, the way you were created—not trying to be something or somebody you're not, but just being *you*! When we get this, the most ridiculous of impossibilities become possible because no longer is it about us, it's about the Rock we're holding onto.

PRAYER

Father, thank you for creating me unique and special and just the way you wanted me to be. Thank you that you know everything about me—my strengths and weaknesses—and still you want to use me as I am. Help me walk confidently as *me*, fully clothed in your armor but no one else's. Help me to be one who takes out the giants in my land by walking with Christ the Rock by my side and the River of God flowing through me at all times. Cause me to be someone who doesn't fear the giants, but rather someone who embraces confidence in who you are inside me. Thank you for your passionate desire to use me to change and save nations. I commit to being the best "me" I can be by the power of your Holy Spirit! Amen!

THOUGHTS/NOTES/REVELATION

8.

OVERCOMING FEAR

One of the greatest things that gets in the way of the sons and daughters of God rising up (to take their positions as sons, with authority) is that big bad wolf called fear. I don't care who you are, timidity and intimidation should *never* stop you from fulfilling your God-given destiny, nor should it stop you from using your authority here on the earth. God's not looking for a bunch of kids with ruling staffs that never use those staffs. He's not looking for kids who have all sorts of gifts but are afraid to pull them out and show off what their Papa gave them. He wants a generation to arise with power and authority to take the kingdom of heaven with force and take dominion in the land. Oftentimes as Christians we let circumstances get the best of us. Instead of keeping our focus on Jesus, we focus on the obstacles in front of us and let fear stand in the way of our breakthroughs.

Part of walking in our God-given authority is taking authority in each situation we come across. Fear is usually what stands in the way of anyone's destiny. Think about the disciples when they were in the boat on the lake. A storm came and the winds shook the boat and the young men around in such a way that panic bombarded those young men (see Luke 8:22-25). Jesus fell asleep in the boat amid the fierce storm that put the whole group in danger. The disciples panicked and woke up Jesus saying, "Master, Master, we are perishing!" Jesus stunned them by rebuking the winds, and when it all died down He

said, "Where is your faith?" This is a great example of Jesus
teaching His followers to walk in authority even in the midst of
crazy situations. We need to learn from this story and grab hold
of crazy wild faith—faith that believes all things are possible,
and faith that relies more on the God of the impossible than on
natural circumstances! This is how my friends and I could take
authority over the rains that were coming at us in Australia (see
chapter one). God's not looking for His kids to put themselves
in dangerous situations, but when situations arise that seem
impossible, He waits for us to do something about them.

Once Jerame and I were scheduled to go to Austin,
Texas, to do a conference. The pastor of the church we were
going to called us up and told us that there was a major hurricane headed straight their way and that the eye of the hurricane
was scheduled to hit them right at the time we were in town.
The pastor courteously asked us if we wanted to cancel the
event and stay home to avoid the hurricane. After praying, we
felt from the Lord that we needed to go there and that God
would change the pattern of the weather. The night we arrived
the pastor, some leaders, and Jerame and I met up in the sanc-
tuary of the church and began to pray. We prayed for the
meetings and then we took authority over the hurricane. We
spoke to the winds and rain and commanded them to go in the
other direction. Within the next day or two, the weather re-
porter announced that though the eye of the hurricane was
supposed to hit the middle of Austin, it somehow redirected
itself and would not come near us. In fact, over the entire
weekend, we didn't even feel any outer effects of the hurricane!
Praise God; but you see, we took authority over a potentially
dangerous situation and the situation obeyed, in the same way
that the winds and storm obeyed Jesus when He took authority
over them. We need to get some confidence and faith and begin
to see God change situations and nations on our behalf.

Overcome

From fear to faith is the only way we, the body of Christ, are going to mature into radiant sons and daughters for the King, truly knowing who our Father is and knowing the inheritance and rights He's given us. The only way to step into authority is through the transforming of the mind. Nothing transforms the mind like the washing of the Word and the infilling of the Holy Spirit. Ephesians 5:26, in reference to Jesus toward His bride, states, "… having cleansed her by the washing of water with the word." And in 4:23, Paul writes to the Ephesians "… that you be renewed in the spirit of your mind." Both of these Scriptures are referring to the purification and redemption of our hearts and minds through Jesus; we can take any old mindset, including one of fear, and know that the washing of the Word renews our mind—taking it from a place of fear and into the faith of God.

More than anything through the pages of this book, I pray that you receive a right revelation of who you are in Christ, and that fear gets booted out of your life and replaced with faith. I believe the mandate of this book is to induce faith. In the dream that I had when the Lord told me to write this book several years ago, God spoke and said he *overcame the world!* That means He overcame fear too!

I grabbed a hold of this revelation when I was filled with the Holy Spirit at age seventeen—my life was transformed. I was filled with boldness and began to walk in a God-given confidence as a daughter of the Lord instead of as the shy, quiet girl I was before. This revelation of sonship is a continual process of development and growth in the Lord, but it is truly vital that we understand our place in the kingdom as sons of God in order to have true confidence before the King.

King David knew who he was in God … or rather, he knew who God was and that God was for him, so who could be against him? Long before David was king, he simply remained faithful to what he was called to do at the given time. As a young boy, he tended his father's sheep. He remained faithful in that even to the point of overcoming obstacles, such as defeating the lion and the bear in order to protect the sheep. When the time came to approach Goliath in public there was no issue, because he'd already been prepared in the secret place. In the same way, we as believers are tested in the secret place so that God can prove himself big enough and powerful through our lives in the major situations. God wants to trust us with nations and changing laws of the land, but how is He going to trust us with these things if He first can't trust us with the one thing He places before us—the greatest test addresses our intimacy and obedience to His voice.

Oftentimes I will be walking through a mall and the Holy Spirit will prompt me to go and prophesy or talk with a worker in one of the stores. If He can trust me to be obedient to these promptings and go be a witness for Him in the little situations, He will surely trust me to be a voice for Him to nations. The closer you get to the Holy Spirit, the more acquainted with His voice you become. The more you spend time with Him in the secret place, the more you'll hear His voice in the public place. There are many encounters waiting for you in the public arena. David was faithful with the sheep placed before him, so God trusted him with armies and people groups. When you're faithful to step out and pray for the one before you, God will trust you to witness to many more.

Let go!
David didn't know he was about to fight a giant and become a hero—even at a young age—but his intimacy with God and his faithfulness and obedience in the small things promoted him to the bigger things. In 1 Samuel 17 we can read the story of David and Goliath: David's father, Jesse, sent David out to the battlefield to bring bread and cheese to his brothers, who were

supposed to be fighting the Philistines; however, when David arrived at the camp he found the Israelites cowering instead of braving the giant! David was shocked that a mere man intimidated God's people.

Body of Christ, we need to get over our intimidation and stand up for what we believe in! We need to step over our fears and trust in the Holy Spirit. "Greater is He who is in you than he who is in the world!" (1 John 4:4). "There is no fear in love; but perfect love casts out fear" (1 John 4:18). "God is *love*" (1 John 4:8), so it's time we embrace love and let go of every fear! I've seen many people set free from fear (both fear of man and fear of the devil), and I can say that I see people freed because He first freed me from that intimidation. I pray great freedom over you from fear!

A love encounter

I was in a church in Scotland recently, when a woman (who rarely responded to needing prayer) walked in at the end of the meeting. She was tormented with fear and shame due to much abuse she'd encountered in life. The woman simply approached me and asked for prayer. I could tell that she was like a little child inside—shy, afraid, and as though she had no father—and I began to show her love (because perfect love is what gets rid of fear; see 1 John 4:18), and then I began to pray. As I began, another voice began to speak through her—not her own. I took authority over the demonic operating through her, but what brought the real freedom was not in the casting out, but the love that was demonstrated. Love mixed with authority is a most powerful weapon, friends, and it is how you will overcome even the hardest of strongholds. When you encounter love, fear melts away.

She then sensed Jesus in a sad situation of her past. Every area of her life began to get touched by the peace of God and be overcome by His voice and by His love. She even began to see angels (in the Spirit), who gave her gifts. This woman encountered the love of God.

Because I was once freed (on a much smaller scale than this, but nonetheless, freed from fear and intimidation), I was able to help someone else get freed. This woman's face changed simply because of her newfound freedom from fear and shame. She went away that night with a new peace in her spirit. I don't know how the woman is doing today, but I do know that she had a real God encounter that night in Scotland, and she was touched by the love of the Father. We are called to be overcomers so that we, too, can help others overcome.

It's time to get out of our boxes and take a risk for Christ. I've heard it said many times that faith equals risk. True statement. David would never have overcome a giant and become a hero had he not taken a step of faith and risked his life, just like Esther. She risked her *life* in hopes that maybe a nation would be saved. God honored her faith and the risk that she took and, as a result, she saved an entire nation from annihilation in a day! She could have turned down that risk and the entire Jewish population would have been put to death. Instead, God used a young lady who put her life on the line and the whole nation was saved. God is looking for risk-takers! He's looking for people who are willing to step out in faith and expect God to move on their behalf in a miraculous way.

Know His voice

Joshua was a man who remained in the presence of the Lord even after Moses came down off the mountain of God. He had such pure intimacy with God that after Moses went on to be with the Lord, Joshua was entrusted with continuing to lead the people, and even lead them into the Promised Land. The number one thing that is highlighted about his life and ministry, though, beginning with Moses's commissioning of Joshua, is the command to be courageous. I believe God is looking for men and women who want His heart and who are willing to step out in faith with courage in ridiculous ways. He is looking for people of faith who will not let fear step in the way of destiny and rob them of their promised lands. Joshua 1:9 says: "Have I not commanded you? Be strong and courageous! Do not tremble or be dismayed, for the Lord your God is with you wherever you go." God *commanded* Joshua! Joshua's leader had just died and he was left to lead an entire people group into an unknown land … yet rather than allow any room for fear, God spoke and said that He was with Joshua, and not to be afraid. The key to Joshua receiving that courage and faith was, I believe, his intimacy with the Lord.

Joshua spent much time on the mountain in prayer. He sought the Lord and thus, he heard the Lord. The way to overcome fear and have faith is through intimacy with God. We must get into God's presence, hear His voice, and know that He is with us! When this becomes a heart revelation, everything will change in our mindsets. Much of the church has been living in a place of deferred hope, which makes the heartsick, or they've let the failures of the past hold them back. The moment Lot's wife and daughters looked back on the land from which they came—the land that was clothed in wickedness—was the moment that they became pillars of salt (see Gen. 19:25-27).

There's no time to look back into the past and stay there. There's no time to go back to old habits and live in old ways. It's time we press on toward the goal to win the prize (see Philipp. 3:13). We need to grab hold of the rod of authority that we've been given, stop fearing it, and take dominion in the land! When Moses was called into "ministry," God asked him during the burning bush experience, "What is it that you have in your hand, [Moses]?" (Exodus 4:2). Moses answered, saying, "A rod." That rod represented Moses's gifting and anointing. He would go on to use it before Pharaoh as a sign/evidence of the supernatural God that Moses served. God has put a rod of authority in your hands. He's given you authority to cast out demons, heal the sick, raise the dead, and cleanse the lepers. He's given you authority to release revelations of a supernatural God on the earth to a generation that is desperate to know what is real. The world is hungry for an encounter. It's time we get over the fear of the authority that God's put in our hands and begin to step out and become the encounter that people are waiting for!

Moses jumped when God told him to throw the rod on the ground and it became a serpent; in fact, he ran from it! He ran from his very own rod! He didn't know what he had until it became something supernatural. Much of the church is like this—we don't know the authority that we've been given, and until we step out and pray for a sick person and see him healed, we won't know the power of God that lies within us. It's like my own walk with the Lord: I loved the Lord with all my heart, soul, and mind, but didn't know the power that lay within me until I had a renewed mind and realized that the miracles of Jesus's day are for *now*. The moment that I caught that revelation, I became unstoppable. All of a sudden I was praying for everything that moved.

People aren't looking for a debate or persuasive words (well, most people aren't), but they *are* looking for an impacting encounter. It's the supernatural that will win this world to God. All over the Muslim world, people are having visions and dreams of Jesus—even physical manifestations of the Christ—and that is what is winning them to God. We can have all the right words and all the best Scriptures (and we definitely do need to know our Scriptures and know the Word—it *is* the very sword that we fight and win battles with), but unless we have the Spirit and power of God, there will be no conviction that leads to salvation and, therefore, there will be no transformation in those we encounter. The Apostle Paul had all the education in the world, but even he said that it wasn't by what he knew, but rather by the power of God that he would declare the good news of Jesus Christ. (Paul to the Corinthians: "And my speech and my preaching were not with persuasive words of human wisdom, but in demonstration of the Spirit and of power, that your faith should not be in the wisdom of men but in the power of God" [1 Cor. 2:4-5].)

PRAYER

Lord, I ask your forgiveness for giving into the temptation of fear and intimidation. Take it away and replace it with courage! Help me to be strong and courageous like you called Joshua to be, and to take the opportunities you place in front of me without cowering back in fear. I am responding to the call of boldness and faith. I receive that faith and courage right now, in the name of Jesus! Amen.

THOUGHTS/NOTES/REVELATION

9.

🏵 GOD OF THE IMPOSSIBLE 🏵

God always does "far more abundantly beyond all that we ask or think" (Ephesians 3:20). It's time we think outside the box and begin to ask God for the greater. I believe we're living in a time and day when the miracles should be far greater than ever before. The Bible says that the latter days will be greater than the former; therefore, there should be greater and more creative miracles and more of the presence of God manifesting on the earth than ever seen in the past.

The glory of God is the presence and person of the Holy Spirit. The more the glory of God manifests on the earth and in the body of Christ, the more His presence will be seen. Where God's presence is, His kingdom is. Where His kingdom is, sickness, disease, fear, pain, and death cannot stand. It's time we pursue His presence like never before so that we become more and more familiar with His heart, mind, and ways. It's then that the creative realm will begin to manifest in and through our lives.

Our amazing God

Time and time again God continues to amaze me. I mean, can you fathom that the God of all creation designed you and me so intricately, so ornately, and that He cares about our every thought and emotion? *And* in that design is a working system? In all of creation, God has and continues to work the impossible, and what we take for granted, He has the brains behind.

Even researchers are continually studying and finding out new stuff about the earth and galaxies, the human body, and the way things work in the world. In the midst of all the unknowns, and behind even the most intelligent discoveries, is a God who truly cares, a God who truly knows the inner workings of each and every thing, each and every body. He truly **is** the God of the impossible. And truly He wants to use you and me to demonstrate that to the world. He wants to become big in you so that His name can become great to the world.

"Thus says the Lord, 'Let not a wise man boast of his wisdom, and let not the mighty man boast of his might, let not a rich man boast of his riches; but let him who boasts boast of this, that he understands and knows Me, that I am the Lord who exercises lovingkindness, justice and righteousness on earth; for I delight in these things,' declares the Lord" (Jeremiah 9:23-24).

When we boast in who God is, God makes himself known. He desires to reveal His justice and lovingkindness to the world, and He will do it through a humble but confident generation of God—seekers who know who they are and whose they are. In a world where there are so many seemingly impossible situations of injustice and unrighteousness, we serve a God who looks lovingly on those situations with eyes of possibility. Will you boast in your God and allow Him to do the impossible through you? Will you call upon His name, stand up in the authority you've been given, and see to it that God gets the glory by showing a world that impossibilities are really only impossible in human eyes? Our limitations as believers must go. We must look to the One who created heaven and earth, knowing that He has just as much creative power now as He did at the beginning of time. That same Creator lives in you and me, and that same Creator longs to create through you and me. Impossibilities are no longer impossible when you know the One who lives inside you.

Think outside the box

Nothing is impossible when you walk in God's authority. We need to start thinking outside the box and begin to make decrees over regions and nations according to God's word and heart. The Bible says "Decree a thing and it will be established for you and light will shine on your ways" (Job 22:28). If this is true, we need to have faith to see mountains moved. I was in Egypt a number of years ago, and there's a mountain there that literally was moved by a Christian who was being threatened and mocked. The mockers said that if the Bible is really true, the man would be able to speak to the mountain and it would move. In faith, the Christian man pointed at the mountain, made a decree, and everyone watched as the mountain shifted and moved over! That was a miracle that got everyone thinking about the reality of God! We need to step up our faith and activate our decrees! It's only as we get into the heart of God and into hearing His voice that we can know what His heart wants to decree. "Faith comes from hearing and hearing by the word of God" (Romans 10:17).

I was getting my hair done in Vancouver, Canada, one afternoon, when my hairdresser told me that she'd battled seizures on a regular/even daily basis ever since she was a little child. My heart beat with compassion for the woman. I'd already seen her healed of a bone injury in the past, so as I went to hug her goodbye, I whispered in her ear, "And be free from seizures, in Jesus's name!" About a month later I returned to the salon to find out that my hairdresser hadn't had a seizure in a month—ever since I'd whispered in her ear! This is the authority that we carry, and you see it operated here by love. I felt compassion, gave a hug and then, using my God-given authority, issued the command for freedom. Perfect love casts out all fear. That day in that salon, perfect love cast out fear and it set a captive free. Love is too powerful to ignore and fear is not worth your time. Let's become overcomers so that we can see others overcome.

Take a risk

Peter heard the word of God. When he responded in faith he saw the miraculous. When Jesus came walking across the water in the fourth watch of the night (see Matthew 14:22-33), the disciples presumed Jesus to be a ghost. The winds were bad and Jesus had seen from the land that the disciples were struggling at the oar. He came walking *on* the water, and the disciples were afraid. They hardly believed it was even Jesus. Impossibility was made possible by God. Peter even said to Jesus, "Lord, if it is really You, command me to come to You on the water." And Jesus responded, "Come!" (Matt 14:28-29). Then Peter got out of the boat and *walked on water*! Peter did the impossible.

By the authority that you've been given in Christ, by His word spoken, you have the power to do the extraordinary. You have the power to do the impossible. It's all about hearing God's word spoken to you and then responding in faith to it. When Peter responded in faith to Jesus's word to him to come, Peter took a step of faith and jumped out of the boat. He was willing to do the unknown. He was willing to put a foot onto that body of water and walk toward the One who called him.

If only Peter would have kept his eyes on Jesus instead of getting distracted by the storm and the waves, he could have walked a lot farther on the water. We need to keep our eyes fixed on Jesus and walk toward His words, in faith. When the situations around us—whether in health or provision or relationship or work—look impossible, we mustn't get caught up in the impossibilities. It is key that we keep our eyes on Jesus, "the author and perfecter of faith" (Hebrews 12:2). When we do this *nothing* will be impossible. When you walk with Him, you will be able to calm the biggest storm and see the most incredible miracle. When it comes down to it, we need simple faith to believe God for the extraordinary. If the Holy Spirit prompts you to pray for someone with a missing kidney, you'd better pray for that person. God is the God of the impossible, and that God is living *inside* you, waiting to do the impossible *through* you. If he says *go,* you'd better go. If He says *pray,* you'd better pray.

Command it

The man standing in front of me was given very little hope by the doctors and, in desperation, he came to a meeting I was ministering in with the expectation of receiving a touch from God. The young musician grabbed my shoulder in the middle of me calling out words of knowledge and said something like this:

"Please, I really need a miracle...."

He interrupted the meeting, but then again, so had the hemorrhaging woman who touched the hem of Jesus's garment. Jesus didn't turn her away; why should I turn this man filled with hunger away? His words moved me to compassion and caused me to instantly take the authority I'd been given by Jesus; I decreed his miracle.

The man had been given only months to live, and he'd been struggling with a collapsed lung all his life. He had had a lung transplant some time before, but even with the transplant, his lung continued to give him problems and it continued to collapse. He literally felt a vibration in his lung every time he took a breath, and he could never breathe in deeply due to having very little lung capacity. I laid a hand on the man and commanded that oxygen flow and the lung be recreated. I took the authority Jesus gave us and used it on a man in a desperate situation.

Instantly the man reported that the vibrations inside his chest (that he always felt when taking in a breath of oxygen) had completely stopped. Not only that, he was able to take his first deep breath ever! The man went home that night, checked his lung capacity on his breathing machine, and discovered that his breathing capacity had gone way up. It continued to go up overnight, and within a couple of days he went for a medical checkup. After the examination the doctor remarked in shock that somehow the man had received a new lung! He marked him down as a medical miracle! This was a man who had been given only months to live, and overnight he received a completely fresh start to life and was given a glorious hope and a future!

God is the God of the impossible. He makes the most impossible situations possible. That's why He's supernatural! You're called to be super-natural. You're called to rise up and shine and be bold and courageous, watching superhero Jesus do the work through *you!* The angel Gabriel didn't come to a married woman and promise the birthing of a Savior; he came to a *virgin* girl named Mary. We all know that it is absolutely impossible for a virgin girl to conceive a baby, but *this* virgin girl had faith. When the angel told her she would be mother to the Son of God, Mary simply said to Gabriel, "How can this be…?" (Luke 1:34), and the angel responded, "The Holy Spirit will come upon you, and the power of the Most High will overshadow you; and for that reason the holy Child shall be called the Son of God." The angel went on to say, "For nothing will be impossible with God" (Luke 1:35-37).

When God speaks creation happens and the supernatural becomes easy. He is longing to show himself strong on behalf of those who diligently seek Him. "For the eyes of the Lord move to and fro throughout the earth that He may strongly support those whose heart is completely His" (2 Chron. 16:9).

PRAYER

Lord, I know that you are the God of the impossible. I know that no matter the circumstance, you can do what I could never even have imagined. Help me believe for the impossible. Help me see through eyes of faith and always keep my eyes fixed on you, the author and perfecter of my faith. I want to be used by you to do the absolutely impossible, live a supernatural lifestyle, and see the supernatural manifest in everyday life in the lives of those I come across. Amen.

THOUGHTS/NOTES/REVELATION

10.

POWER OF THE SPIRIT

Recently I've had several dreams in which the Spirit of God came on me in power and I blurted out in the language of the Holy Spirit—in the gift of tongues—as a demonstration of the power of God. I wasn't planning to speak out in my heavenly language; it just happened. Holy Spirit came on me and released His power and presence through the supernatural. In all of these dreams (about three of them), each person that I came across—one was a Buddhist, one was a Jehovah's Witness, and one was a New Age man involved in occult practices—encountered the reality of Christ Jesus when I operated out of the power and authority of the Holy Spirit.

People in the world are looking for an encounter with reality—they're looking for the truth. It's our job to show them that reality; it's our job to show them the power of the Holy Spirit and the authority of Christ. Paul writes to the Corinthians that his "message and [his] preaching were not in persuasive words of wisdom, but in demonstration of the Spirit and of power, so that [their] faith would not rest on the wisdom of men, but on the power of God" (1 Cor. 2:4). Even though Paul had a history of studying the Law and Scriptures—even from before his salvation, when he was persecuting the church—he was not as concerned about the words that he spoke when witnessing, but rather in the power of the Spirit being released. Paul understood that though some people might believe through mere words, most people would be moved at the demonstration of the Spirit of God. For this very reason it is important that we become so filled with the Spirit of God that His power is able to move freely through us. If witches and warlocks are demonstrating a type of power, how much more should we as believers—having the same Spirit that raised Christ Jesus from the dead (see Rom. 8:11) dwelling inside us—operate in *true* power.

We talked about the difference between authority and power in an earlier chapter, and it is important that we understand that difference, but we need to know that by the Holy Spirit we have the greatest power of all. That's why we should not only be walking in the power of the Holy Spirit, but in the outright authority that Jesus commissioned us with. Power comes with the gift of salvation and the Holy Spirit; authority comes from a place of trust and intimacy. As I mentioned earlier, God tests our hearts through obedience to His word and to His voice. When we obey the promptings of the Holy Spirit on a small scale, He can trust us with so much more (see Luke 16:10). It's like this with authority. When we're faithful to obey the commands regarding small issues, God knows that we'll be faithful with major issues; therefore, He puts weight behind our words and weight on our decrees.

Step out

God so honors hunger and willingness to take risks and be bold that He will give you grace and empower you to have fruit if you're just willing. That's what happened with me. I was willing, and the Lord saw my motivation and hunger and I had incredible favor that helped people to get healed, touched, saved, and delivered. The Holy Spirit is looking for willing individuals that He can partner with to see God's kingdom come on the earth. It's not hard for God the Father to step out of heaven, touch the earth, and save every person in an instant—or even to change situations of injustice on the earth in an instant.

The reason why God doesn't do this, though, is because He *so* wants to co-labor with His bride to see a generation touched by the love and power of God. Not only that, He is a God of free choice. He gives us the right to choose love or reject it, He gives us the right to choose Him or reject Him, and He gives us the right to choose to be used by Him or to sit back as dormant Christians (which is what the devil wants).

It's time for the body of Christ to arise with confidence in the God in whom they put their trust. It's time for us as believers to step out in boldness and in the power of the Spirit to see people like those in my recent dreams—shocked at the power and reality of God. When I blurted out in tongues— a gift given by the Holy Spirit (see 1 Cor.12:10)—the Buddhist man suddenly changed his facial expression to one of utter amazement at the reality of Christ. He had a revelation when the power of the Spirit was manifested. It opened up conversation for me to begin to speak to him about the healing power of Christ. When I encountered the New Age waiter in another dream, the moment I blurted out in tongues and prophecy, he immediately became alarmed and disappeared. The *true* kind of supernatural intimidated the man who had a *false* kind of supernatural. When I encountered the seemingly overpowering Jehovah's Witness lady, and simply blurted out in confidence who I was and then spoke in tongues and immediately went into words of knowledge and wisdom about her life and condition, she immediately backed off and looked like she'd been struck by lightning because the reality of God hit her. We *need* the power of God. We *need* the filling of the Holy Spirit. You will not be completely successful in your witnessing tactics unless you've first been baptized in the Holy Spirit.

Ever since I was a young teenager, I had a desire to witness. Even when I was that shy, timid girl in high school, I still had a desire to make Jesus known. The problem was, I didn't have boldness; I didn't have confidence, and I didn't have the power of the Holy Spirit. We *need* the power of the Holy Spirit and the gift of tongues. This is what will strengthen your inner man. This is what will give you the power to witness, and not only to witness, but to be successful in your witnessing. We want fruit that remains, that leaves an unforgettable mark on a generation. When the power and presence of God touches a person, he goes away marked. Whether or not that person chooses to receive salvation in the moment, when you touch someone with the power of the Holy Spirit, he will continually recall that day. It could be what becomes the making or breaking encounter of a person's life—one that propels him toward full freedom and salvation.

We're in the family

Oftentimes we may feel inadequate or insufficient and believe that we can't be used by God because of situations or weaknesses in our lives. The truth of the matter is this: God is simply looking for willing vessels. He's looking for individuals who have a heart after Him and a heart for people, and on these individuals He will pour out His Spirit. This is our inheritance. *We are no longer orphans. We are sons: sons of the kingdom.*

> *For you have not received a spirit of slavery leading to fear again, but you have received a spirit of adoption as sons by which we cry out, 'Abba! Father!' The Spirit Himself testifies with our spirit that we are children of God, and if children, heirs also, heirs of God and fellow heirs with Christ...* (Romans 8:15-17).

It's time we throw off fearfulness and embrace the Spirit of God! The moment the new Christians in the book of Acts embraced the baptism of the Holy Spirit, not only did they speak in new tongues, they were also baptized in boldness! Peter, who was a timid and insecure guy in the past, a guy who even denied Jesus at the cross, was filled with the Holy Spirit on the day of Pentecost and began to preach the gospel of Jesus Christ with boldness and conviction! This is the power of God! This is what we need to begin to embrace: the Spirit of adoption and the Spirit of transformation—the Holy Spirit. If we let intimidation and fear of man hold us back, we'll never accomplish anything for the kingdom. Matthew 11:12 says: "And from the days of John the Baptist until now the kingdom of heaven suffers violence, and violent men take it by force." What is being said here is that it is only those who have passion and tenacity who take hold of the kingdom of heaven and bring restoration to the earth.

I've found in my years of being a witness for the King that the more one is bold in stepping out and being used by Him, the more the motivation is there, and the more the grace for impact is there. I challenge you to get bold and begin to step out and make an impact and, of course, be led by the Holy Spirit. That's really what this life is about—friendship with the Holy Spirit. When you walk with the awareness that God is with you *always* and *everywhere* you go (see Josh. 1:9 and Matt. 28:20), you will begin to hear His voice that much more, and you will begin to be led by Him more and more.

How do you go about being filled with and led by the Holy Spirit? *Ask!* Jesus said to His disciples, "If you ask Me anything in My name, I will do it" (John 14:14). And Jesus went on to say, "I will ask the Father, and He will give you another Helper, that He may be with you forever" (v. 16). If you want the Holy Spirit to fill your life and fill you with power from on high, simply ask the Father in the name of Jesus. God "will not leave us as orphans" (v.18), but will leave us a Helper—the Holy Spirit. Jesus commanded the disciples to wait for the promise of the Father (see Acts 1:4). We too must ask and wait for the empowering of the Holy Spirit so that we can know Jesus intimately and also become fruitful witnesses!

PRAYER

Jesus, I want to be filled with your Spirit. Please rest and remain on me and empower me with your Holy Spirit. Make me one who so carries your presence that even the hardest of hearts would see your reality. Cause me to be led and moved by your Spirit, always demonstrating the power of your Spirit to a generation that doesn't know you. I ask this in the precious name of Jesus. Amen!

THOUGHTS/NOTES/REVELATION

THOUGHTS/NOTES/REVELATION

11.

🀛 POWER OF COMPASSION 🀛

Nothing brings greater joy than leaving an impact of love and transformation in a person's life. If ever I have been down and discouraged and then been out in the marketplace and had a divine appointment in which I got to pray and see a healing, or I impacted someone with love through a prophetic/encouraging word, my day was instantly turned around for the good. It's so true that it's better to give than to receive. You give someone love and in return you feel that love. Step out and love!

Greater love

Jesus said, "he who believes in Me, the works that I do, he will do also; and greater works than these he will do; because I go to the Father" (John 14:12). He was speaking to believers. He continued on and said that it was so that the Father would be glorified. Everything Jesus did was out of intimacy with the Father and compassion for the people. Jesus saw remarkable signs and wonders, and it was:

1. because he was intimate and obedient to the Father and he walked in his identity as a son, and

2. because he had genuine love for the people.

Jesus moved out of compassion and then miracles took place. It's time we get deep into the heart of the Father, seeking

Him to know Him and to know His heart. His heart is love.

A few years ago I had a significant encounter with the heart of God. During worship one night I was taken in the Spirit into the very heart of God. I began to see down the corridors and into the different chambers of His heart. In one room were the broken and injured, in another room the orphan and widow. Different people were in each of the different parts of His heart. I was broken over the tangible love I saw and felt for each group of people. From that point on, the Lord really began to show me what it means to have His compassion and His heart for the world around me. He began to show me how power is rooted in love. God is love, and His power comes out of the core of who He is: *love*.

I believe it's time we begin to cry out for His heart and begin to operate out of that place of love and compassion. Yes, we need to know our authority so we know what kind of power is available to those who believe, but then we must carry His heart to see a harvest come forth. Love is what changes a generation. We will see greater works if we operate out of love as opposed to greed. We're not trying to get brownie points or gold stars in the kingdom. It's not time to put another notch in the belt; it's time to walk in humility and be motivated by His heart. All of our boasts must be in the Lord and who He is, not what we can do. (Psalm 34:2: "My soul will make its boast in the Lord; the humble will hear it and rejoice.") God opposes the proud but gives grace to the humble. When we walk in true humility (which is utter dependence on Christ and the Holy Spirit), we can't help but see the greater works of Christ unfold. He pours out grace (empowerment and enablement) on those who put their trust in Him. Lean upon the Rock and He will pour out water. Trust in the Lord and He will pour out His Spirit and you will see the power of God displayed.

At the same time, love the people and creative miracles will take place. Jesus modeled this. In Mark 1:40-42 we read about a leper who came to Jesus begging for his miracle. Lepers were the outcasts of society, the ones no one would love on and the ones no one would go near. This leper came in boldness to the only one he knew could heal him and the only one he knew who modeled love to the rejects of society. And my Jesus was *moved with and motivated by compassion*. Jesus felt God's heart and real love for this man that no one else in society would love. As a result, when Jesus reached out and touched the man, the man was instantly cleansed and the leprosy left him. That's an incredible miracle. Compassion moves the heart of God to manifest His love and power. If you want to walk in a greater level of the authority of God and see a greater breakthrough with the power of God operating in your life, get compassion.

The heart of God

How do you get compassion? Get into the heart of God. How do you get into the heart of God? Spend time in His presence. As I mentioned previously, Joshua spent time in the presence of the Lord—he spent time in the secret place of the Most High and as a result, he was the one commissioned to lead the people of God into the Promised Land. In the same way, when you spend time in the presence of the King, you're forever changed. When you spend time in worship, prayer, and thanksgiving, as well as in the Word of God, you become more and more like Him. A huge part of His likeness is His love. That love manifests through compassion for the hurting, lost, and dying. As you're transformed more and more into His likeness, you get His heart, you learn His heart, and you begin to take hold of the promises of God ... that includes walking in your God-given authority as a believer.

We are heirs of the kingdom and "fellow heirs with Christ" (Romans 8:17). Our inheritance is His presence. Our inheritance is also His rod of authority. He trusts those with a heart for Him, and He trusts those with a heart for His people.

Love is the key. Love is the answer to a lost and dying generation. When you're motivated by love, you can't help but be bold. The love of God causes you to do things you would never ordinarily do.

My husband was in Africa some years ago, and when he took a group with him through a particular village, he was moved by the Spirit of God to go into a certain home. Before he could enter, though, the interpreter stopped him and said,

"Jerame, this is the home of a witchdoctor. Are you sure you want to go inside this home?"

Jerame told the guide, "Absolutely! God is going to touch this man's life!"

My husband was moved by a compelling compassion that was about to bring a major miracle into the witchdoctor's life. As he led the little team into the witchdoctor's home, the guide informed the team that the man had gangrene. Jerame saw that the witchdoctor's leg had been completely eaten away by this dreadful disease. Puss and slime were pouring out of the pores of his skin, and without thinking—but being motivated by love and by the Spirit of God—Jerame grabbed hold of the man's leg (gangrene goo and all!), and began to pray for a revelation of the love and reality of Jesus to grip the man. He stepped out in his *authority* as a son of God, took authority over the disease, and blessed the man. No one knew what happened after that until Jerame was back in Africa a year later. The pastor/interpreter who had accompanied Jerame on the previous trip informed my husband that the witchdoctor woke up the next morning completely healed of gangrene, and had shown up at the church to get saved. At this point in time, the man was being discipled and trained for the position of pastoral leadership! That's an incredible miracle! It all happened because one individual was moved with compassion and knew his authority in Christ, got bold, and decided to be radically obedient to the Spirit of God.

The supernatural manifests when we're obedient to the Spirit of God and when we have compassion on the people we are dealing with. The supernatural manifests when we know the authority and power we carry, but in true humility carry the heart of God into a situation and see the person through the eyes of love. Every time Jesus looked at a situation with eyes of love, the nature of heaven manifested. Every time Jesus saw through the Father's heart of compassion and also made a declaration (a command out of authority), a miracle took place.

Drawn by compassion

I was on vacation one time in Antigua (an island country in the Caribbean), and as we drove through the local market place, I couldn't help but feel love and a compelling compassion for the people. We were with a group of pastors, and because we were on our way to the beach, there was no way I could just stop the van and get out to minister there. On the way back, however, I shared my heart with Jerame—how I earnestly desired to minister love and hope to the people who clearly had so much need—and so we began to move in and out of the local market, witnessing to people. All of a sudden, on this so-called vacation, people were being healed and touched by the love of God.

There was one little boy in particular who really caught my attention—he was around the age of eight and was selling peanuts. He noticed that my eyes were drawn to him and he began to approach me. I could tell something was wrong with his right eye and when I asked him what had happened, he responded by telling me that he'd been blind in that eye since he was a baby. I told him that I see miracles and that I'd like to pray for him. The boy allowed me to put a hand over his eye and we began to pray and decree. We decreed that the boy's eye be restored, in Jesus's name. When we took our hands off the boy's eye, he saw perfectly for the first time since he could remember! With grace and ease, the boy began to tell us how many fingers we were holding up, and he was able to pinpoint details through his healed eye that were completely impossible to see prior to that prayer of authority and release of compassion. Simply on a pleasurable vacation, we were part of releasing the power and love of God in a region, even to the point of seeing a blind eye open! The boy nearly cried, he was so touched by the love of God. He said he was already a believer, but he'd never known the power of God like that before.

Jesus always impacted regions through compassion, and he transformed lives through love and authority. We have that same authority and we *can* have that same love—if we just get into the heart of God and spend time in His presence. Not only did Jesus heal the sick through compassion, he ministered life and power through compassion. Yes, healing and creative miracles take place through power that comes from compassion, but so do supernatural signs and wonders. All sorts of supernatural signs manifest through a heart of compassion if we're just open to being used by God. We need to look outside the box.

Take a look at when Jesus fed the five thousand (in Mark 6): Jesus's disciples were tired and ready to rest, but Jesus saw a multitude of people waiting for Him to come down from the mountain so they could hear Him speak. Although I'm sure the disciples were ready to call it quits for the day and simply chill out and have fun with Jesus, the Lord had mercy on the people. Jesus was "moved with compassion for them, because they were like sheep not having a shepherd" (Mark 6:34, NKJV). Because of the compassion he felt for the people, he began to teach them and lead them, and from there a supernatural miracle took place. When the disciples told Jesus that it was dinnertime and he should send the people on their way, Jesus's response was shocking: "You give them something to eat" (Mark 6:37). The disciples were shocked and explained (as if Jesus didn't realize himself) that there were five thousand men there! Jesus didn't seem to mind because he knew the authority that he was walking under— the authority of his Father in heaven, who owns the cattle on a thousand hills—and he felt the love and compassion of the heart of His Father toward the people. This said, Jesus took what he could get—which ended up being five loaves of bread and two fish, and he blessed them, broke them, and gave them to the disciples to give out.

As they gave the food out that was now blessed with Jesus's heart of compassion, the loaves and fish multiplied and somehow fed every person in attendance. The compassion of Jesus multiplied the bread and the loaves to the point of demonstrating the love and power of God to His disciples and everyone around Him. Not only was there just enough to feed the five thousand (plus their wives and children, so He may have easily fed up to fifteen thousand), there were twelve baskets left over! When we move out of compassion and offer ourselves wholly to the Lord, He will not only take what we have and multiply it, He will do exceedingly greater than we could ever ask or think.

PRAYER

Father, give me a heart after you. Let me experience, know, and feel your very heart of love and compassion. Let me walk in the authority you've given me, but keep me always motivated by your love, by your heart. Help me see through eyes of love. Help me see people the way you see them. Today I commit to loving people in the best way possible. I commit to looking to you and seeing through the lens of Jesus. May compassion compel me, Lord. I ask this in the name of Jesus. Amen.

THOUGHTS/NOTES/REVELATION

12.

❧ RISE UP ❧

It's time for us, the children of God, to rise up in faith and confidence and serve God's purpose for us: to bring peace, joy, and righteousness to a lost and hurting world. It's time for us to bring healing and hope where there's pain and death, and to bring restoration where there's brokenness. The mandate has been given; it's time to fulfill it! "All authority in heaven and earth has been given to Me […], go therefore!" (Matt. 28: 18-19). Jesus said it, released it, and mandated us to go and do the same.

We need to get into His word (the Bible), meditate on what He says, and then go for it. Again, Romans 10:17 says "faith comes from hearing, and hearing by the word of Christ." Meditate on His word and you won't be able to help but get faith. You won't be able to help but catch His authority. Then *rise up!* Heal the sick! Make a declaration and watch the miraculous manifest! It's time we start believing in the authority God has given us and start walking it out. It's not too hard for God to save a nation in a day, and the truth of the matter is that He wants to use *you!* Let's partner with God to see movements happen and regions changed! If Ezekiel could call life to dry dead bones (see Ezek. 37) and that was Old Testament news, how much more should we use our authority to call forth life to dry places and freedom to the oppressed?

Partner with God
God is looking for willing available vessels. It doesn't matter

where you are, if you're out "doing evangelism" or just going about your day, or even if you're on vacation; the kingdom of heaven is at hand *everywhere* and *always*. Anyone who grabs hold of it will see nations changed. Authority is yours, by the grace of God. Jesus has commissioned you! You have been called; will you step out and take hold of the mandate?

We need to get out of our comfort zones and begin to have eyes to see what the Holy Spirit is looking at and ears to hear what He is asking us to do. When you're willing you'll find that divine opportunities will pop up wherever you are. It's a matter of what you're focused on. Are you focused on yourself or are you focused on God and on loving people? If you're only focused on yourself, you'll only look at your own needs and what *you* have in mind to do in a day. If you're focused on God, you'll be attentive to His voice and leading, and you'll see opportunities that you absolutely would not have seen if you were not looking to Him and His heart. As well, if you're focused on loving people, you'll see the needs in an area and will move to demonstrate the love and power of God instead of just looking at them with hopelessness.

When you know the authority and power that lies within you, and you know that Christ in you *is* the hope of glory (see Col. 1:27), you will look at people and situations with new vision, knowing that you *are* the answer to their very need. Whether it's a healing, provision, salvation, joy, freedom, or whatever their need may be, you are the answer to their hope. When we get this evangelism becomes easy. When we get this, stepping out in love and power no longer becomes something we have to *do*, but rather it becomes a lifestyle of passion.

Revival on vacation

Jerame and I were on a year-end birthday vacation a few years ago and we had a stop in Cartagena, Colombia, for a day. Though we were scheduled to take part in a guided tour of the old part of the Spanish colonial city, our hearts, along with the

Holy Spirit, had different plans. We ended up doing our walk around the city with a guide and then breaking off and scouting out a personal interpreter. When a Colombian with very good English approached us to sell us jewelry, we asked him if we could pay him twenty dollars to translate for us for about an hour and a half. The man instantly agreed, as that was more money than he usually made in a whole day of work.

We saw this as a prime opportunity to witness the love of Jesus in a place that had a lot of need. For a number of years already I'd had dreams of Colombia, and even prophetic words about it, and knew that God had purpose in us being there even while we were on vacation. We asked the man to take us out of the touristy area and into the locals' market. The man was excited, but didn't really know what was going on. It was amazing because God turned the situation into a powerful time of loving people and demonstrating His reality and love and power to people. Once we got into the local market, the man still didn't quite understand what we were about to do, but he completely agreed to translate everything we would say word for word.

We began to ask people if they needed miracles, and with so much need and such soft hearts, people began to respond. Immediately off the bat people began to be healed. There was a man with some sort of a crippled and painful arm, and by the power of God and a simple decree in love, the pain totally left and his arm was healed and stretched out! There was a woman working a fruit stand who had tremendous pain in her knees. She could hardly move them, and after declaring healing over her, she stood up and started shouting, "Halleluiah! Halleluiah!" and dancing all around! All the pain left her and she was overjoyed with the love and power of God touching her! Her friend across the way, also working a fruit stand, needed a miracle as well. After praying for her, she too was healed. By this point, our translator was so excited about the power of God that he began to shout down the streets, asking who needed a miracle! We were having revival on vacation!

We carried on during this vacation/mission to Colombia and next came across a couple in a park. The man needed healing in his kidneys. After praying for him, all pain left and both he and his wife received Jesus into their hearts for the first time! By this point, our interpreter was insisting we come pray for his friend's business, knowing that if we prayed God would bless it. [Do you know that this is true? When the people of God speak blessing over people and places, the blessing of the Lord remains! In the same way, when we speak a curse, a curse remains. When we begin to walk in this authority, people will be coming to us for the answers *and* for the blessing of God. That's why this man wanted us to bless his friend's business. Rise up!] So we blessed the jewelry business and in return, the owner of the shop gave me a small pendant for a necklace as a sign of gratitude for what she knew was deposited in her jewelry shop when we came to pray. When we sow love, we reap love and honor back.

Just before we arrived back to the Old City where we were supposed to meet back up with our tour group, we came across another one of our interpreter's friends. This particular man had a hernia and jumped on the opportunity to be prayed for. After laying hands on him and making a decree for healing, the man excitedly told us that all pain was gone and that he was healed. Our interpreter was so excited about the fruit of the day that he was set on fire. We planned on leading him to the Lord, but discovered he was already a Christian but had never seen the power of God like that before. From that point on, he intended to pray for the sick and expect miracles. He also wished we had more time so he could take us to his home and family. You see, this is love in motion. We weren't "scheduled" to minister, nor did we have an "evangelism day" set up, but we were sensitive to the Holy Spirit and sensitive to love and compassion and, as a result, we saw a city impacted in a day. Not only that, it was a day that we were supposedly on vacation. In my opinion, this kind of a day is so much more rewarding and joy-filled than an ordinary vacation day. Seeing God manifest His love and power through you is one of the most rewarding and satisfying feelings one can experience. There is nothing like it.

Rise up!

Rise up, friends! Take hold of the kingdom of heaven at hand! Take hold of your authority! We need to have our eyes opened and begin to look at people and places and situations through the knowing lens that we are the very essence of hope that they are crying out for. We'll see cities transformed if we simply get this heart and passion. It's Jesus's passion. His passion is to love; his passion is for compassion. He sent his disciples out two by two and the testimonies that came back were remarkable. Jesus sent the disciples out and commissioned them with authority over unclean spirits. They went out preaching the gospel, calling people to repentance, casting out demons, and healing the sick (see Mark 6:7-13), just like Jesus. This is the work that we are called to do.

Acts 10:38 says: "You know of Jesus of Nazareth, how God anointed Him with the Holy Spirit and with power, and how He went about doing good and healing all who were oppressed by the devil, for God was with Him." Jesus has commissioned us with this same authority and mandate. Just like His disciples did (see Mark 6), and just as it says that Jesus did in Acts 10:38, *we* are His disciples. *We* are called to *rise up* and do good! *We* are called to heal the sick and broken and set the captives free. It's time to shine. It's time we do what the Bible says we will do—greater works than even Jesus did (John 14:12). It's time we begin to see a move of God happen through our lives everywhere we go!

PRAYER

God, I want to be used by you! Take me, mold me, use me for your glory. I give myself to you. Help me to arise and shine, taking hold of the mandate you've called me to as a son/daughter of yours. I want to rise up and see you glorified through my life. Set divine opportunities before me in which I get to manifest your kingdom to the world. Let me be a spark plug for a move of your Spirit here on the earth. In Jesus's name, amen!

THOUGHTS/NOTES/REVELATION

THOUGHTS/NOTES/REVELATION

13.

HIS ROAR

Jesus said to the disciples before His ascension, "All authority has been given to Me in heaven and on earth. Go therefore and make disciples of all the nations, baptizing them in the name of the Father and of the Son and of the Holy Spirit, teaching them to observe all things that I have commanded you; and lo, I am with you always, even to the end of the age." (Matt. 28:18-20). Here's the paraphrased key: All authority has been given to Me ... so *go*!

Jesus commanded us to walk in the authority He gave us. We all know this is the Great Commission. We're released. What happened in the Bible was not reserved just for the days of the Bible. I think sometimes people get deceived into thinking that Jesus did it but that it's not for us to do today. Wrong. God is the same yesterday, today, and forever, and He commanded us to take the gospel and the *full* kingdom message to the world. It is our *mandate* to release the authority Jesus commissioned us with.

In Mark 16:17 Jesus said, "These signs will accompany those who have believed: in My name they will cast out demons, they will speak with new tongues; they will pick up serpents, and if they drink any deadly poison, it will not hurt them; they will lay hands on the sick, and they will recover." We don't need to live in fear; we need to live in faith. We need to live by the very Word of God. Jesus said to heal the sick, so heal the sick! Jesus said to cast out demons, so cast out demons!

Jesus said to raise the dead, so bring life to the spiritually dead, and if an opportunity arises for you to pray for someone who has died before her time, speak life into that body! (see Matt. 10:8, "Heal the sick, *raise the dead*, cleanse the lepers, cast out demons …") Do what Jesus asked us to do! We're called to be in this world but not *of* this world. God is looking for a people who will stand up and be bold for Him and lead the "blind" into the *light* of His glory.

Authority of the Lion

During worship recently the Lord gave me a vision—I saw the face of a lion, the Lion of the Tribe of Judah. He was calm and confident, with eyes of peace. I knew He was simply releasing a peace and confidence into the midst of any storm people could be going through. Then the vision shifted.

This same lion came out of a cave with a small lion cub in his mouth, striding in confidence and pride. He walked to the edge of a cliff that reminded me of the Disney movie *The Lion King*—the scene in which Mufasa came out to the edge of Pride Rock with his small lion cub, Simba. In this vision, though, instead of Rafiki taking Simba and holding him up to the rest of the animal kingdom (to announce the birth of the prince), the Lion of Judah himself stood on the edge of the rock with the lion cub, ready to show him off to the rest of the world.

On another occasion, but also in the midst of a worship atmosphere in Singapore, the Lord appeared to me in a vision in the midst of the room. I only saw His face and His beautiful brown hair, which was blowing back softly like the thick mane of a lion. As I watched His hair blow, no longer did I see His face, but rather I saw the face of a lion. His thick brown locks truly did turn into a mane of golden hues on a lion. At that moment I knew that God was going to release the authority of heaven in the service because the authority of heaven had shown up. Sure enough, after I preached many remarkable miracles took place and, most importantly, salvation took place.

Ultimate authority

Jesus—the Lion of the Tribe of Judah—is longing to show His bride off to the rest of the world. Lions represent authority. In the animal kingdom, it's the lion's roar that goes out and shakes the ground, and all creation listens. In the animal kingdom, the lion carries the authority and respect of all the creation around him. Jesus is the risen King, and He is reigning with ultimate authority as the Lion of Judah.

The Father longs to show His children off to the rest of the world. You are the Father's pride. You are the one He longs to show off by your demonstration of His authority to the rest of the kingdoms of this earth. It's time to lift our heads and look into the face of the Lion. It's time we look into those eyes of peaceful confidence and receive His peace so that we might release that peace and confidence into every storm. Let's receive the pride of God and boast in Him.

Receiving the pride of God doesn't mean boasting in yourself. True humility is knowing who you are and knowing who God is in you. Receiving the pride of God means boasting in who He is! When you boast in Him, you empower Him to be God and to be supernatural. When you boast in Him, you enable Him to release His kingdom and kingly authority. "The testimony of Jesus is the spirit of prophecy" (Rev 19:10), and the more we boast in God and testify of what He's done for us and those around us, the more we will see Him do. When you testify of a miracle of healing or provision, it releases the faith, power, and authority for another to receive that healing or provision. As the Lion of Judah's pride is in you, may your pride be in God—confident that He can do all things and assured that He is able to do more than we deem possible (see Ephesians 3:20). He wants to show you off to the world, that the world might know that He is God and that He is alive!

> **If you are ready to see the miraculous and you are willing to step out, God *will* use you in great and powerful ways! Let's begin to throw off fear and step out in courage—becoming like Esther, who approached the king's throne with boldness. Let's begin to take what we've been given—our own armor, like David—and face the giants. Take them out simply by being you and partnering with Jesus in authority. It's time to rise up and become that army God is awakening! Grab hold of that rod of authority and let's take dominion!**

We've been talking about the authority of God. All throughout this book I've been sharing true and (many) documented stories of the power of God. I've been challenging you, the reader, to begin to step into your place in the kingdom of God and step out in your authority as a son or daughter of the King. The one thing I must mention before I finish this book is that you must know Jesus Christ as lord and savior of your life to begin to walk in the power and authority that I've been talking about.

If you have never committed your life and heart to Jesus as the God of your life, I invite you to do so now. I've been sharing story after story of the power and miraculous healing touch of Jesus, and this is the reality of Jesus: He loves you. He desires to reveal himself to you in such a real and tangible way, and He longs for you to walk in this incredible authority and power that I've been talking about. *First*, though, you must commit your heart and life to Jesus, the Son of God. If you accept this invitation to receive the greatest miracle and greatest gift of all—the gift of salvation which sets us free from the hold of death and hell and sin and sickness, and releases freedom, healing, and abundant life to you, with an eternal reward of heaven—then I invite you to pray this simple prayer from the depth of your heart:

PRAYER
Dear Jesus, I believe in you. I believe you died and rose again
to save me from my sin and to set me free. Today I choose
you. Come into my heart and be lord and savior of my life. Fill
me with your Holy Spirit and teach me to walk in your ways.
Thank you for saving me and thank you for calling me one of
yours, a child of God; in Jesus's name, amen.

Now you are a child of God! This is the greatest miracle
of all. Now you can walk in this incredible authority and power
that I have been talking about through the pages of this book.
You are free, you are a child of the King, and authority is at
your hand!

THOUGHTS/NOTES/REVELATION

❊ ABOUT THE AUTHOR ❊

Miranda Nelson is a prophetic revivalist who is passionate about equipping others to demonstrate the kingdom through a faith-filled, intimate, and uncompromising walk with the Father. Miranda lives with her husband Jerame in Pasadena, California, and together they travel the world teaching, preaching, and releasing the supernatural power of God. Miranda loves life, and when she's not on the conference circuit she spends her time modeling, painting, traveling, and exploring the great outdoors.

E-mail: admin@livingathisfeet.org
Website: www.livingathisfeet.org

OTHER TEACHING MATERIALS
BY MIRANDA NELSON

The Rest of God

DVD

Through supernatural experiences and visitations she's had with the Lord, as well as through the Word, Miranda teaches keys on entering the promises of God and moving into our inheritance as sons and daughters of the King.

$12.00

The Armor of God

DVD

Miranda teaches what it looks like to "put on the full armor of God" (Ephesians 6), and what the weapons of our warfare are. She teaches on the power of the high praises of God, and how strongholds come down as we worship the Lord.

$12.00

Wisdom's Call

DVD

Through personal experiences, as well as biblical examples, Miranda teaches how the fear of the Lord and yearning for real godly wisdom releases the supernatural in every area of your life.

$12.00

OTHER TEACHING MATERIALS
BY MIRANDA NELSON

Fire of God's Love

DVD

In this three-part series you will receive understanding on how to position yourself to receive everything God has for you regarding the supernatural and His power. This teaching set will equip you to walk in a greater ability of seeing and hearing from God in the Spirit, and it will also teach you how to walk in God's power in your everyday life.

1. Marked by the Fire of God's Love – Jerame Nelson
2. The Fire of Wisdom & Revelation – Jerame Nelson
3. Fire and Glory – Miranda Nelson

$25.00

Find all these DVDs at Living at His Feet Publications' store: https://www.livingathisfeet.org/store/index.php/dvds.html

Printed in Australia
AUOC02n0930061114
264156AU00005B/9/P

9 780984 968794